# THE
# ANCIENT
# ROMANS

Other titles in the *Lost Civilizations* series include:

The Ancient Greeks
The Ancient Egyptians
Empires of Mesopotamia
The Mayans

# LOST CIVILIZATIONS

# THE ANCIENT ROMANS

Don Nardo

LUCENT BOOKS
P.O. BOX 289011
SAN DIEGO, CA 92198-9011

J
937

Library of Congress Cataloging-in-Publication Data

Nardo, Don, 1947–
    The ancient Romans / by Don Nardo
        p. cm. — (Lost Civilizations)
        Includes bibliographical references and index.
        Summary: Discusses the civilization of ancient Rome, including its founding and
early centuries, its high point, social classes and institutions, aspects of daily life, its
eventual decline and fall, and the enduring legacy of Rome.
        ISBN 1-56006-706-3 (hardcover : alk. paper)
        1. Rome—Civilization—Juvenile literature. [1. Rome—Civilization.]
I. Title. II. Lost Civilizations (San Diego, Calif.).
    DG77 .N28 2001
    937—dc21

                                                                                        00-008650

Copyright © 2001 by Lucent Books, Inc.
P.O. Box 289011, San Diego, CA 92198-9011
Printed in the U.S.A.

55438

# Contents

# FOREWORD

"What marvel is this?" asked the noted eighteenth-century German poet and philosopher, Friedrich Schiller. "O earth . . . what is your lap sending forth? Is there life in the deeps as well? A race yet unknown hiding under the lava?" The "marvel" that excited Schiller was the discovery, in the early 1700s, of two entire ancient Roman cities buried beneath over sixty feet of hardened volcanic ash and lava near the modern city of Naples, on Italy's western coast. "Ancient Pompeii is found again!" Schiller joyfully exclaimed. "And the city of Hercules rises!"

People had known about the existence of long lost civilizations before Schiller's day, of course. Stonehenge, a circle of huge, very ancient stones had stood, silent and mysterious, on a plain in Britain as long as people could remember. And the ruins of temples and other structures erected by the ancient inhabitants of Egypt, Palestine, Greece, and Rome had for untold centuries sprawled in magnificent profusion throughout the Mediterranean world. But when, why, and how were these monuments built? And what were the exact histories and beliefs of the peoples who built them? A few scattered surviving ancient literary texts had provided some partial answers to some of these questions. But not until Pompeii and Herculaneum started to emerge from the ashes did the modern world begin to study and re-construct lost civilizations in a systematic manner.

Even then, the process was at first slow and uncertain. Pompeii, a bustling, prosperous town of some twenty thousand inhabitants, and the smaller Herculaneum met their doom on August 24, A.D. 79, when the nearby volcano, Mt. Vesuvius, blew its top and literally erased them from the map. For nearly seventeen centuries, their contents, preserved in a massive cocoon of volcanic debris, rested undisturbed. Not until the early eighteenth century did people begin raising statues and other artifacts from the buried cities; and at first this was done in a haphazard, unscientific manner. The diggers, who were seeking art treasures to adorn their gardens and mansions, gave no thought to the historical value of the finds. The sad fact was that at the time no trained experts existed to dig up and study lost civilizations in a proper manner.

This unfortunate situation began to change in 1763. In that year, Johann J. Winckelmann, a German librarian fascinated by antiquities (the name then used for ancient artifacts), began to investigate Pompeii and Herculaneum. Although he made some mistakes and drew some wrong conclusions, Winckelmann laid the initial, crucial groundwork for a new science—archaeology (a term derived from two Greek words meaning "to talk about ancient things.")

His book, *History of the Art of Antiquity*, became a model for the first generation of archaeologists to follow in their efforts to understand other lost civilizations. "With unerring sensitivity," noted scholar C. W. Ceram explains, "Winckelmann groped toward original insights, and expressed them with such power of language that the cultured European world was carried away by a wave of enthusiasm for the antique ideal. This . . . was of prime importance in shaping the course of archaeology in the following century. It demonstrated means of understanding ancient cultures through their artifacts."

In the two centuries that followed, archaeologists, historians, and other scholars began to piece together the remains of lost civilizations around the world. The glory that was Greece, the grandeur that was Rome, the cradles of human civilization in Egypt's Nile valley and Mesopotamia's Tigris-Euphrates valley, the colorful royal court of ancient China's Han Dynasty, the mysterious stone cities of the Maya and Aztec in Central America—all of these and many more were revealed in fascinating, often startling, if sometimes incomplete detail by the romantic adventure of archaeological research. This work, which continues, is vital. "Digs are in progress all over the world," says Ceram. "For we need to understand the past five thousand years in order to master the next hundred years."

Each volume in the *Lost Civilizations* series examines the history, works, everyday life, and importance of ancient cultures. The archaeological discoveries and methods used to gather this knowledge are stressed throughout. Where possible, quotes by the ancients themselves, and also by later historians, archaeologists, and other experts support and enliven the text. Primary and secondary sources are carefully documented by footnotes and each volume supplies the reader with an extensive Works Consulted list. These and other research tools, including glossaries and time lines, afford the reader a thorough understanding of how a civilization that was long lost has once more seen the light of day and begun to reveal its secrets to its captivated modern descendants.

# INTRODUCTION

# THE
# SURVIVING EVIDENCE
# OF A GREAT PEOPLE

Of all the lost ancient civilizations, historians know more about ancient Rome than any other. This is partly because Roman culture was extremely long-lived. At least as early as the seventh century B.C., a small city-state called Rome existed near the western Italian coast, a tiny realm that was at first ruled by kings and then in the late sixth century B.C. instituted a republican form of government. Over the next several centuries, the Roman Republic aggressively expanded far beyond Italy's borders and by a mixture of conquest, intimidation, and diplomacy absorbed all of the lands ringing the Mediterranean Sea. Eventually, Rome's republican system became outmoded and unstable. But its collapse did not bring about Rome's end. Instead, the state was transformed into the autocratic Roman Empire, a mighty realm that for several more centuries dominated most of the Mediterranean world.

Finally, in the fifth and sixth centuries A.D., that empire disintegrated. Yet a part of Rome still lived on, for it was only the western portion of the realm that had fallen; the eastern part survived for almost another thousand years as the Byzantine Empire (which, though it became more Greek in character, still preserved many Roman customs and institutions). In the west, meanwhile, many Roman customs and ideas survived and helped profoundly to shape the emerging nations of Europe. Thus, only the most physical, tangible aspects of Roman civilization were lost. And in a very real way, as suggested by the late, noted scholar R. H. Barrow, Rome never fell but, rather, "turned into something else. Rome, superseded as the source of political power, passed into even greater supremacy as an idea; Rome, with the Latin language [became] immortal."[1]

Indeed, during the many centuries of their existence as a people, the Romans created (or borrowed from others) a large number of political, social, and literary ideas and institutions. And not surprisingly, they generated a great deal of material evidence of their achievements, beliefs, and everyday customs and habits. Much of this evidence did not survive the ravages of time, to be sure, and most of what did survive is random, disorganized, and in varying states of preservation, ranging from good to poor. Also, some time periods of the Roman saga are represented far better than others. Very little substantial evidence survives for the Monarchy (roughly spanning the eighth through sixth centuries B.C.), for instance, or for the early Republic. And there are regrettable gaps in the historical record throughout the rest of Rome's long tenure as a living, breathing culture. This is because, as century after century came and went, the destructive effects of war, vandalism, neglect, and natural deterioration all took their toll. Yet even though more than 90 percent of the vestiges of Roman civilization have disappeared forever, the sheer bulk of the artifacts that remain is enormous; this fact constitutes an enduring testimonial to Rome's importance in the ancient world and to the size and magnificence of its overall achievement.

This evidence documenting Roman history, life, and culture takes various forms. First, there are the written sources. These include the works of Roman historians, including Livy (59 B.C.–A.D. 17), who wrote a massive history of Rome up to his time (of the work's 142 books, 35 plus some fragments of the others survive); Tacitus (ca.

A.D. 55–ca. 120), who chronicled the lives of the Empire's early rulers in his *Annals* and *Histories*; and Ammianus (ca. A.D. 330–395), who wrote in detail about the leaders, politics, and wars of his own century. Ammianus also made some valuable observations of ordinary people. "Of the lowest and poorest class," he wrote, for example,

> some spend the night in bars, others shelter under the awnings of the theaters. . . . They hold quarrelsome gambling sessions, at which they make ugly noises by breathing loudly through the nose; or else . . . they wear themselves out from dawn to dusk. . . in detailed discussion of the merits and demerits of [race] horses and their drivers.[2]

Some of the gaps left by these and other Roman historians were filled by the works of Greek writers, notably the historian Polybius

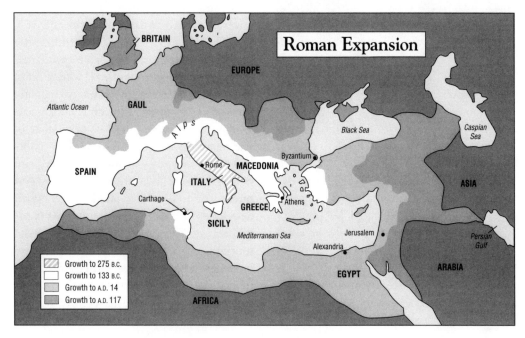

Roman Expansion

(ca. 200–ca. 118 B.C.), who recorded the events of the Second and Third Punic Wars (in which Rome fought Carthage, a prosperous maritime empire centered in north Africa), and the biographer and moralist Plutarch (ca. A.D. 46–ca. 126), whose numerous biographies of leading Romans remain precious mines of information.

Other crucial written sources include the surviving works of Roman poets, encyclopedists, jurists, playwrights, orators, philosophers, statesmen, and others. One of the greatest of them all, the statesman and orator Marcus Tullius Cicero (106–43 B.C.), generated a huge literary output, of which fifty-eight lengthy speeches, more than eight

hundred letters, and some two thousand pages of philosophical and rhetorical tracts survive. These works constitute a virtual treasure trove of information about Cicero himself (in fact, more is known about him than any other person of the ancient world), his friends, his society, and the Roman character, both real and ideal. Regarding the latter, he wrote that the best possible public servant

> should carry with [him] greatness of spirit and. . . lead a dignified and self-consistent life. . . . If anyone is entering public life, let him beware of thinking only of the honor that it brings. . . . At the same time, let him take care not to lose heart too readily through discouragement nor yet to be overconfident through ambition.[3]

The vastness of Cicero's output aside, any classical historian will attest that the surviving written sources are often vague, incomplete, and/or misleading and do not begin to cover all aspects of Roman history and daily life. This forces scholars to try to fill in the gaps by examining inscriptions, artifacts, and other archaeological evidence. One kind of inscription, the tomb epitaph, is particularly important because it is often the principal source of knowledge about the lives, feelings, and relationships of those who had no political power or voice—women, children, and slaves. "My one and only wife," reads an epitaph found in Gaul (Roman France). "With a loving spirit, she lived faithful to her faithful husband, always optimistic, even in bitter times, she never shirked her duties."[4]

Other archaeological evidence includes artifacts such as tools, utensils, jewelry, weapons, coins, and the remains of buildings and animal and human skeletons; bronze or

*Cicero, greatest of all Roman orators, whose writings modern historians find invaluable.*

*Pictured here are some of the ruins of the Roman town of Pompeii. The volcanic material that encased it during the eruption of* A.D. *79 preserved a good deal of its contents.*

stone sculptures such as those that adorned Roman temples, which typically picture the gods, sacred processions, and other religious themes; and paintings on vases, cups, and walls, which depict sports and games, music and dance, sexual activities, eating and drinking, clothing styles, armor and warfare, and much more. Excavations of the famous cities of Pompeii and Herculaneum, for example, which were buried by a volcanic eruption in A.D. 79, have yielded many such buildings, statues, paintings, and other artifacts in an excellent state of preservation. In the words of scholar Maurizio Forte, Pompeii is a site

> in chronological suspension—"frozen in time." . . . What is emerging from archaeological research allows a partial reconstruction of the most obscure aspects of the daily life of the

period. For example, excavation in [a former apartment block] has uncovered a kitchen with a dramatically complete assemblage of all the objects and materials used to prepare a hot meal.[5]

Unfortunately, few archaeological sites are as complete and well preserved as Pompeii. But rapidly improving excavation techniques, enhanced by computer imaging and other advanced and cutting-edge technology, allow researchers to deduce a great deal from minimal, damaged, or crumbling artifacts.

Combining all of these kinds of evidence, scholars have pieced together a still incomplete but nevertheless vivid and fascinating picture of one of the world's greatest and most pivotal civilizations. The great Livy was quite sincere when he wrote in the preface of his masterwork,

*First-century* B.C. *historian Livy, who wrote a detailed history of Rome.*

I hope my passion for Rome's past has not impaired my judgment; for I do honestly believe that no country has ever been greater or purer than ours or richer in good citizens and noble deeds; none has been free for so many generations from the vices of avarice [greed] and luxury; nowhere have thrift and plain living been for so long held in such esteem.[6]

Expressing similar sentiments, his contemporary, the poet Ovid, extended Rome's reach into a limitless future: "The city of our sons and sons of sons, greater than any city we have known, or has been known or shall be known to men."[7] Livy and Ovid can be forgiven for exaggerating out of love for their country and an unabashed awe for its great works. Even allowing for such distortion, however, their evaluations were not far off the mark. The truth is that few peoples have had so profound an influence on so many generations in so many diverse lands. Rome, "the eternal city," remains, and will likely always remain, one of the cornerstones of Western culture.

# CHAPTER ONE

# THE FOUNDING OF ROME: LEGENDS VERSUS EVIDENCE

The exact origins of Rome, the Romans, and the early events of their long and auspicious saga are lost, perhaps forever, in the mists of time. This uncertainty is a modern development, of course. If we could go back to the first century B.C., when Roman civilization was nearing its zenith, and ask an average Roman about such matters, he or she would likely have a ready and confident answer. The great city of Rome was founded sometime in the middle of the eighth century B.C., he or she would say, by the hero Romulus, who subsequently became its first king. (It was during the first century B.C. that Roman scholars tried to arrive at an exact founding date. This was very difficult because the Romans had used several different calendars and dating systems over the centuries and there were omissions in and inconsistencies among them. The date 753 B.C., which eventually became the most widely accepted, was based on calculations made by the noted scholar Marcus Terentius Varro, who died in 27 B.C.[8]) For the Romans, therefore, the matter of their origins was a fairly simple matter. In their view, their history and much of their culture sprang into being at the time of Rome's founding, as described in their proud and colorful national mythology.

What the Romans did not know, and modern scholars do, is that early Roman culture did not appear suddenly but, rather, developed slowly over the course of many centuries. Archaeology has revealed that the group of Latin-speaking tribes to which the Romans belonged lived in Italy long before the eighth century B.C. Moreover, there was likely no single, purposeful founding of Rome; rather, the city's site was long occupied by primitive villages that gradually coalesced to form one town. In a sense, that town subsequently became many, since succeeding generations tended to build new buildings on top of older ones. In the process, important past relics were repeatedly erased, forgotten, or entered what classical scholar Claude Moatti calls "the veil of legend."[9] Integral to that veil's fabric, the Roman founding myths may well have been based on garbled memories of real people and events from Rome's earliest centuries. So as they continue to unearth new knowledge about these obscure times, archaeologists and historians remain mindful that Roman mythology and history are probably intricately intertwined in ways that are still not well understood.

## Creating a Link to Ancient Heroes

There are two beginnings to Rome's story, therefore—the one accepted by the ancient Romans themselves and the one revealed by the spades of modern excavators—each of which must be considered in the context of the other. In their own version, the Romans, like all peoples in all ages, wanted to believe that they were descended from characters of

heroic stature. They early took note that the Greeks, whose culture they admired and eagerly absorbed, looked back with pride to their ancestors' exploits in the remote and legendary "Age of Heroes."[10] Especially important to the Greeks was the Trojan War. In this epic tale, later immortalized by the Greek poet Homer in his *Iliad*, a number of early Greek kings banded together in an expedition against the trading city of Troy (on the northwestern coast of Asia Minor, what is now Turkey). After a ten-year siege they sacked the city and recovered Helen, a Greek queen who had been abducted by a Trojan prince. The heroes of the war—the Greeks Achilles and Odysseus and the Trojans Hector and Aeneas,

## WERE THE ROMANS REALLY TROJANS?

Here, from his masterful study *The Beginnings of Rome*, historian T. J. Cornell speculates about why the Romans accepted and perpetuated the idea that they were descended from the Trojan prince Aeneas.

"In general it is not surprising that the Romans were willing to embrace a story that flattered their pride by associating them with the legendary traditions of the Greeks, whose cultural superiority they were forced to acknowledge—albeit sometimes grudgingly. More specifically, in Greek myth Aeneas possessed qualities which the Romans liked to see in themselves, such as reverence for the gods and love of his fatherland. The Trojan legend was also useful to the Romans in that it gave them a respectable identity in the eyes of a wider world, and one that could be used to advantage in their dealings with the Greeks. . . . Finally, we should note that by claiming to be Trojans the Romans were saying that they were not Greeks, and in a sense defining themselves in opposition to the Greeks. . . . In the hands of Virgil and other writers of the first century B.C. it became a means to reconcile them, and make Roman rule acceptable in the Greek world."

for example—were seen as men of larger-than-life stature who accomplished deeds of incredible valor and interacted with the gods.

When Greek settlers began establishing cities in southern Italy in the late 700s and early 600s B.C., they brought their legends of the Trojan War with them. The early Romans, who inhabited a nearby small patch of central Italy, soon had sporadic contact with the more culturally advanced visitors and were duly impressed. Perhaps because they had no ancestral heroes of their own who quite compared in stature with those who fought at Troy, the Romans attempted to create a link between themselves and one of the leading characters of the Trojan story. At least by the sixth century B.C., it appears, Roman legends had incorporated the tale of the Trojan prince Aeneas's escape from the burning Troy and his fateful journey to Italy.

After many dangerous and colorful adventures, so the story goes in *The Aeneid*, an epic poem composed by the first-century-B.C. Roman writer Virgil, Aeneas sailed to Cumae in southern Italy. A prophet had earlier told him to seek out the Sibyl, a wise woman who could see into the future. The Sibyl greeted him and told him that he was destined to fight a war in Italy over the right to marry an Italian bride. Aeneas then begged her to help him find a way into the underworld so that he might once more see his beloved father, Anchises, who had died during the journey across the Mediterranean. Granting the request, the Sibyl led Aeneas down into the underworld, and in time they found the spirit of the old man.

After their reunion, the father offered to show the son the future of the grand and blessed race Aeneas would sire. "Come then," said Anchises, "I shall show you the

*This Renaissance sculpture depicts Aeneas carrying his father, Anchises, from the burning Troy.*

whole span of our destiny." First, he revealed, Aeneas's offspring would found the city of Alba Longa in the Italian region of Latium (lying south of the Tiber River); the line of Alba's noble rulers would lead to Romulus, who himself would establish a city—none other than Rome. "Under his tutelage," Anchises predicted, "our glorious Rome shall rule the whole wide world [and] her spirit shall match the spirit of the gods."[11] Anchises showed his son the long line of noble Romans, finally culminating in the greatest of them all, Augustus Caesar, who was destined to bring about a new golden age for Rome and humanity.

After Aeneas and the Sibyl returned from their journey through the lower depths, the hero traveled northward to Latium to fulfill the destiny that had been revealed to him. He met the local ruler, Latinus, and soon sought the hand of that king's daughter, Lavinia. But Turnus, the prince of a neighboring people called the Rutulians, had already asked for Lavinia's hand, and the rivalry over Lavinia soon led to a terrible war, thus fulfilling the Sibyl's prophecy that Aeneas would fight over an Italian bride.

Eventually, Aeneas defeated Turnus and married Lavinia. And from the union of the Trojan and Latin races, fulfilling the destiny ordained by Jupiter (leader of the gods), sprang the lineage that would lead to the noble Romans, who would one day rule all the world. For the Romans, Jupiter had earlier told Venus (goddess of love), "I see no measure nor date [and] I grant them dominion without end . . . the master-race, the wearers of the Toga."[12]

## The Legend of Romulus

In this way—through family lineage—the Romans tied Romulus, the hero of their most popular local founding legend, to Aeneas. Romulus and his twin brother, Remus, were supposedly members of the royal house of Alba Longa. When they were infants, their great-uncle, who usurped the throne, ordered them to be drowned in the Tiber, but they fortunately washed ashore, where a she-wolf fed them and some poor shepherds eventually took them in. When the brothers grew to

*A nineteenth-century woodcut captures the drama of the legendary battle between the Trojan prince Aeneas and the Italian leader Turnus. After defeating Turnus, Aeneas supposedly went on to found the Roman race.*

manhood and learned their true identities, they returned to Alba, overthrew their great-uncle, and restored their grandfather, the rightful king, to his throne. Then they set out to establish a new city of their own on the northern edge of the Latium plain.

As it turned out, however, Romulus ended up founding the city by himself, for he and Remus got into a petty squabble, fought, and Romulus slew his brother. Shortly after this tragedy, Romulus laid the new town's initial foundations, as told by Plutarch in his *Life of Romulus*:

> Romulus, having buried his brother Remus . . . set to building his city; and sent for men out of Tuscany [then Etruria, homeland of the Etruscans], who directed him . . . in all the ceremonies to be observed, as in a religious rite. First, they dug a round trench . . . and into it solemnly threw the first-fruits of all things either good by custom or necessary by nature; lastly, every man taking a small piece of earth of the country from whence he came, they all threw [the piece] in randomly together. Making this trench . . . their center, they laid out the boundary of the city in a circle round it. Then the founder fitted to a plow a metal plowshare [blade], and, yoking together a bull and a cow, drove himself a deep line or furrow round the boundary. . . . With this line they laid out the [city] wall [on the Palatine, one of Rome's famed seven hills]; and where they designed to make a gate, there they . . . left a space. . . . As for the day they began to build the city, it is universally agreed to have been the twenty-first

of April, and that day the Romans annually keep holy, calling it their country's birthday. At first, they say, they sacrificed [to the gods] no living creature on this day, thinking it fit to preserve the feast of their country's birthday pure and without stain of blood.[13]

Once he had established Rome, Romulus proceeded immediately to deal with some important religious, legal, and social matters. According to Livy, after building his wall on the Palatine,

> he offered sacrifice to the gods. . . . Having performed with proper ceremony his religious duties, he summoned his subjects and gave them laws. . . . Meanwhile Rome was growing. . . . To help fill his big new town, [Romulus] threw open . . . a place of asylum for fugitives. Hither fled for refuge all the [outcasts] from the neighboring peoples; some free, some slaves, and all of them wanting nothing more than a fresh start.[14]

Romulus's welcoming of foreigners into the city, like the non-Italian origins of Aeneas, was among later Roman attempts to explain the cosmopolitan nature of their state. As noted scholar T. J. Cornell explains:

> The Roman foundation legend provides evidence, first and foremost, of how the Romans of later times chose to see themselves. . . . The most revealing sign of this is the way it defines the identity of the Roman people as a mixture of different ethnic groups, and of Roman culture as the product of various foreign influences.

# THE QUARREL BETWEEN ROMULUS AND REMUS

In his version of the Roman founding myth, Livy included the following account (translated by Aubrey de Sélincourt in *The Norton Book of Classical Literature*) of the quarrel that led to Remus's death and his brother's establishment of the eternal city.

"Romulus and Remus [after a successful struggle for recognition as rightful members of Alba Longa's royal house] . . . were suddenly seized by an urge to found a new settlement on the spot where they had been left to drown as infants and had been subsequently brought up. . . . Unhappily, the brothers' plans for the future were marred by . . . jealousy and ambition. A disgraceful quarrel arose from a matter in itself trivial. As the brothers were twins and all questions of seniority were therefore precluded, they determined to ask the gods of the countryside to declare by augury [omens, symbolic signs] which of them should govern the new town once it was founded, and give his name to it. . . . Remus, the story goes, was the first to receive a sign—six vultures; and no sooner was this made known to the people than double the number of birds appeared to Romulus. The followers of each promptly saluted their masters as king. . . . Angry words ensued, followed all too soon by blows, and in the course of the affray Remus was killed. There is another story, a commoner one, according to which Remus, by way of jeering at his brother, jumped over the half-built walls of the new settlement, whereupon Romulus killed him in a fit of rage, adding the threat, 'So perish whoever else shall overleap my battlements.' This, then, was how Romulus obtained the sole power. The newly built city was called by its founder's name."

*This famous statue depicts Romulus and Remus as babies being suckled by a wolf.*

*The sixteenth-century Italian painter Giuseppe Cesari created this fresco showing Romulus directing his followers in laying out the boundaries of the "eternal" city of Rome.*

. . . The Roman saga was characteristic of a people who had built up their power by extending their citizenship and continuously admitting new elements into their midst.[15]

## Recent Archaeological Discoveries

How do the events of these foundation myths square with the discoveries made in Italy by modern excavators? First, in the 1930s, the remains of the bases of some primitive huts were discovered on the Palatine and tentatively dated to the eighth century B.C. Both the site and period are the same as those

mentioned in the chief myth of Romulus. Furthermore, more recently, archaeologists have found evidence that one particular hut remained in good repair during the late Republic and on into the Empire, coexisting with, rather than being replaced by, larger stone buildings that rose around it. Surviving ancient literary texts mention a shrine that contained the "House of Romulus," a small hut that the state maintained and to which Romans came periodically to pay homage. It was so highly venerated, in fact, that Augustus, the first emperor, built his own house nearby, no doubt hoping to promote his image by close identification with the city's founder. It seems likely that the hut unearthed recently from definitive proof that Rome was established at that time. Archaeologists have determined beyond a doubt that the Palatine and some of the other nearby Roman hills were inhabited long before—at least by 1000 B.C. and likely a good deal earlier. The evidence consists of graves containing urns filled with the ashes of the cremated inhabitants, accompanied by pottery and bronze utensils and other artifacts. The urns were molded in the shape of huts much like those discovered elsewhere on the Palatine, suggesting that villages made up of such huts existed on the site in the late second millennium B.C.

## Native Italians or Outsiders?

Scholars are not sure of the identity and origins of these early inhabitants of the site of Rome. On the one hand, they may have been native to central Italy, an offshoot of what historians term the "Apennine culture," named after the rugged mountain range that runs north-south through the Italian "boot." This Bronze Age society (characterized by the use of tools and weapons made of bronze), which practiced inhumation (burial of the dead), lasted from about 1800 to 1200 B.C. According to Cornell,

*Pictured are some of the ruins atop Rome's Palatine hill, site of several imperial palaces.*

and the one from the ancient shrine are one and the same. Also, in 1988 excavators found the remains of a fortification wall, dating from the eighth century B.C. as well, on the edge of the Palatine. Was this the wall that Romulus built?

Though at first glance these discoveries appear to corroborate the particulars of the founding legend, scholars remain skeptical. First, there is no way to tell when the Romans set up the Romulus shrine. They may well have discovered the hut's remains later when digging the foundation of some new building, merely speculated that it was the founder's abode, and on this flimsy basis turned it into a shrine.

More important, the fact that the huts and wall date from the eighth century B.C. is far

> The primary economy was based at least in part on transhumant pastoralism—that is, on a form of stock-raising that entails seasonal movement of flocks to upland pastures in the early summer and back to the lowlands again in the autumn. The custom has been traditional in Italy since time immemorial and is still practiced today. It used to be thought that the economy of the Apennine culture was exclusively pastoral, and that the population was

nomadic. But . . . [recent] excavations have revealed permanently settled villages on defensive hilltop sites, with a mixed economy based on . . . agriculture . . . as well as transhumance.[16]

If members of the Apennine culture did indeed settle the Roman hills in the second millennium B.C., their society underwent significant changes during the transition from the Bronze Age to the Iron Age (ca. 1200–900 B.C., during which iron tools and weapons came into use). In much of central and northern Italy during these years, population increases occurred, which may have resulted from higher agricultural yields made possible by the spread of more advanced metalworking techniques. Also, the custom of inhumation was largely replaced by cremation. These changes may have been the

# CREMATION VERSUS INHUMATION

Gravesites and their contents are among the chief kinds of archaeological evidence surviving from early cultures. In this excerpt from his widely read *History of Rome*, noted historian Michael Grant discusses the two main funerary methods used by the settlers of the Latium plain and the Roman hills in the early Iron Age: cremation, in which the body is burned, and inhumation, in which it is buried.

"Cremation and inhumation, the two types of internment characteristic of the two groups of Iron-Age settlers, are both found [in the vicinity of Rome]. The cremators dug small, deep, circular pits within which they placed large globular jars that had stone slats as lids. Inside the jars were urns in which the burned ashes of the dead person were laid. Often the urn was a little model of one of the huts in which the people themselves lived—a design which seems to have originated in Latium. As for the inhumers, they buried the bodies in hollowed-out logs or rough stone sarcophaguses [coffins], which they laid in long rectangular pits or trenches sometimes lined with stones. Cremation and inhumation are sometimes found side by side on Roman sites and even, on occasion, in such close proximity that graves of the two kinds actually cut into one another. But whether the practitioners of these two customs differed from one another in race we cannot say. All that is safe to conjecture from these first Iron Age cemeteries in Rome is that the two groups, whoever they were, gradually mixed . . . both with each other and with whatever sparse populations they already found living on the hilltops when they arrived."

result of cultural influences filtering in from outside Italy and steadily altering its way of life.

Another possibility, one long favored by a number of historians, is that the Latin-speaking tribes who gave rise to the Romans migrated into Italy sometime in the second millennium. The traditional view was that they came in waves across the Alps; however, studies of the distribution of early Italian languages have led some scholars to conclude that at least some early migrants moved southwestward through the Balkans and crossed the Adriatic Sea into eastern Italy. In this scenario, they moved a little at a time across the peninsula; one group settled on the plain of Latium, and some of its members eventually erected villages on one or more of the Roman hills.

Certainly they were not the only group drawn to Rome's unique and commanding site, which provided not only easily defensible hilltops interspersed with rolling farmland but also convenient access to the Tiber (and via it the sea) and trade routes into the Apennines. Livy's assertion that Romulus welcomed many neighboring peoples into the city is based, at least in the general sense, in reality. Members of tribes from all over western Italy arrived in the eighth and seventh centuries B.C. Among them, for example, were the Sabines, from the Apennine foothills, who buried their dead in coffins made of logs; they settled on the Esquiline hill, which lies northeast of the Palatine.

## The Emergence of the Roman City-State

Wherever the original inhabitants of the area came from, it appears that the separate villages on the seven hills coalesced into a single town and became a city-state in the late eighth century at the earliest and more credibly in the early to mid–seventh century B.C. It is probably the distant but durable memory of this event that the later Romans identified with the founding by Romulus. The merger of the villages was, after all, very likely accompanied by much ceremony and the establishment of new and distinct traditions, especially religious ones. "Some of the most ancient religious festivals of later Rome probably go back to this period," wrote the late distinguished scholar Chester G. Starr.

One of these was the primitive fertility rite of the Luperci [priests who annually sacrificed a dog and several goats in the Lupercal, the cave on the Palatine in which the she-wolf supposedly suckled Romulus and Remus] who ran about unclad on February 15 each year; another was the ceremony of the Palilia on April 21 [the date on which Romulus supposedly established the city], which was designed to protect the livestock of the community as it went out to summer pastures. At least a religious union of all the villages in the area is suggested by the traditional festival of the Septimontium [on December 11, held to honor Rome's seven hills and their inhabitants, both previous and present].[17]

It is unknown whether the religious union of the villages and their political union were separate events or whether they occurred at the same time. What seems fairly certain, however, is that the Roman Monarchy came into being some time in the century that followed. The early kings ruled over a relatively small area, probably consisting of no more than a few dozen square miles, most of it uninhabited farmland, swamps, and forests. At the time, no one could have guessed that this tiny city-state, one among hundreds in Italy, would one day come to rule the entire Mediterranean world and leave a permanent cultural imprint on societies around the globe.

# CHAPTER TWO

# ROME'S EARLY CENTURIES: PHENOMENAL SUCCESS AT A PRICE

The first two stages of Rome's existence as a nation-state—the Monarchy and the Republic—were periods of growth and expansion, as the Romans seemingly relentlessly extended their power and influence and conquered most of the Mediterranean world. These early years also witnessed a constant influx of new ideas, social customs, artistic styles, and so on from other peoples. In fact, one of the Romans' most characteristic traits was their talent for imitating others, an ability to borrow the best attributes of foreign cultures and to adapt these to their own special needs. The first-century-B.C. Roman historian Sallust described this talent of his ancestors, saying that they

> were never too proud to take over a sound institution from another country. . . . In short, if they thought anything that an ally or an enemy had was likely to suit them, they enthusiastically adopted it at Rome; for they would rather copy a good thing than be consumed with envy because they had not got it.[18]

The foreign cultures the Romans imitated most were those of the Greeks and the Etruscans (an Italian people who lived in Etruria, the region directly north of Rome), both of whom they eventually conquered and absorbed.

Even though they were ever open to change and improvement, the Romans remained, throughout the centuries of the Republic, conservative and tradition-oriented. They looked back with special pride on the great, often legendary soldiers and statesmen who had shaped early Rome and the memory of the extraordinary stature and deeds of these past heroes remained an inspiration to later Romans. "Rome stands firm upon the values and the men of old," stated the third-century-B.C. Roman writer, Quintus Ennius.[19] And Sallust expanded on this thought, saying about "the good old days,"

> In peace and war . . . virtue was held in high esteem. The closest unity prevailed, and greed was a thing almost unknown. Justice and righteousness were upheld not so much by law as by

natural instinct. . . . In time of war . . . few ever ventured to desert their standards [emblems of their units] or to give ground when hard-pressed. In peace, they governed by conferring benefits on their subjects, not by intimidation; and when wronged they would rather pardon than seek vengeance.[20]

Though this vision of Rome's past was more ideal than real, it became an accepted part of the national consciousness. Over time, the Romans came to see themselves as a singular, even superior, people who had a divine destiny to bring order to and/or rule over others. Their unusual ability to blend an openness to new ideas with a reverence for the past and tradition endowed the early Romans with a unique combination of flexibility and strength. And this proved to be a major key to success in their rise to Mediterranean mastery.

## Rome in the Days of the Kings

That mastery did not come quickly or easily, however. Even after Rome became a city-state and acquired a formal government headed by a king, the central town long remained a small, unimposing place with dirty, unpaved streets lined with timber huts with thatched roofs. The few larger buildings—temples and communal meeting places—were smaller than later versions and still constructed of wood. Most traces of these early structures were erased over the centuries that followed as larger, more durable buildings were erected in their places. During the days of the kings and well into republican times, most Romans did not live in this urban center but dwelled instead in simple huts in the surrounding countryside, hardy shepherds and farmers living a rustic, uncultured existence.

The exact length of the monarchial period, as well as the number of kings and the lengths of their reigns, is unknown. According to later tradition, there were seven kings, beginning with Romulus, who supposedly reigned from 753 to 717 B.C. He was then succeeded by Numa Pompilius, Tullus Hostilius, Ancus

A *third-century* B.C. *bronze figurine depicts an Etruscan man wearing a toga.*

*Rome's second king, Numa Pompilius, urges his people to be devout and industrious.*

Marcius, Tarquinius Priscus, Servius Tullius, and Tarquinius Superbus (or "Tarquin the Proud"). Some of these rulers, especially the first three, were likely legendary rather than real persons, although the last four may well have been real. In any case, recent scholarship suggests that the period of the Monarchy was shorter than tradition held. Also, there may well have been more than seven kings, some of whose identities and deeds merged with those of the traditional seven in historical accounts fashioned centuries later.

The way these rulers were chosen, and how much power and authority they held, is uncertain. But traditions recorded by Livy and other later writers suggest that some kind of election was held in which selected male citizens, probably those who could af-

ford to bear weapons, met periodically in an assembly and either chose or ratified nominees. More important, those chosen had to be ratified by the heads of the leading families, the so-called Roman fathers (*patres*). They made up a privileged social class—the patricians—who would, as senators and military leaders, exercise profound authority and influence over Roman society for many centuries to come. These fathers granted the Assembly "supreme power," Livy wrote, "but on the condition that their election of a king should be valid only if it were ratified by themselves—thus keeping, in effect, as much power as they gave."[21]

Not much is known for sure about Rome's history during the Monarchy. What is certain is that the Romans were frequently in conflict with their immediate neighbors and that Roman territory steadily expanded outward, especially into the Latium plain in the south. For instance, heroic myths, some of which may be exaggerated versions of real events, tell of Rome's takeover of Alba Longa, the region in which the legendary Aeneas had supposedly settled centuries before. In one of the most famous tales, attributed to the reign of Tullus Hostilius (673–642 B.C.), the Romans and Albans were at war. But they wanted to conserve their manpower to fight their common enemy—the Etruscans—so the two sides each chose three champions who would fight to decide the war's outcome. Though two of the three Romans, members of a noble family, the Horatii, were killed, the third was ultimately victorious. "The cheering ranks of the Roman army," Livy recalled, "welcomed back their champion. . . . Alba was subject now to her Roman mistress."[22]

## The Etruscans and Rome

As for that common enemy, the Etruscans, the Romans evidently fought them at intervals over a span of several centuries. All the while, especially at times when relations between the two peoples were cordial, the inhabitants of Rome felt the cultural influence of these more advanced neighbors. The Etruscans were an energetic, talented, highly civilized people who lived in well-fortified cities featuring paved streets laid out in logical, convenient grid patterns. Most of what is known about them comes from excavations of their tombs, which began in earnest in the nineteenth century. Later, in the twentieth century, thousands of Etruscan tombs were discovered using advanced archaeological devices. (These include magnetometers, which measure the intensity of the earth's magnetic field and reveal the presence of ditches, foundations, and other human-made structures lying underground; potentiometers, which reveal underground structures by passing electrical currents through the soil; and periscopes, tubes containing small lights and cameras that excavators lower into the soil.) In one area alone—Tarquinii (a few miles northwest of Rome)—archaeologists found more than five thousand Etruscan tombs in the 1960s. Many of those explored have revealed beautiful wall paintings, sculptures, weapons, pottery, and other grave goods, all providing evidence of a culture that both impressed and inspired the Romans.

*A large number of surviving Etruscan sculptures adorn the tops of sarcophagi (stone coffins). This one shows a well-to-do matron.*

27

*This European fresco, created in the early 1500s, depicts Tarquin the Proud laying the first stones for the Temple of Jupiter on the Capitoline hill.*

Indeed, the Etruscans imparted to the Romans various artistic styles and skills, architectural ideas (such as the arch, which later became a Roman trademark), and certain religious, legal, and political concepts, as well as the "sport" of gladiators fighting to the death. Partly in imitation of Etruscan cities such as Veii (about ten miles north of Rome), in the late sixth century B.C. Rome began its transformation from a crude, ramshackle town to one with stone sewers, a paved forum (main square), and some stone public buildings. The most imposing of these early structures was the first of Rome's temples to its chief god, Jupiter, the construction of which, Livy tells us, was supervised by Rome's last king, Tarquin the Proud:

> The project involved the use not only of public funds but also of a large number of laborers from the poorer classes. The work was hard in itself, and came in addition to their regular military duties; but it was an honorable burden with a solemn religious significance, and they were not, on the whole, unwilling to bear it.[23]

The Etruscans may also have had a hand in ending Tarquin's rule—and with it the Roman Monarchy. Though a great builder, Tarquin, himself of Etruscan birth, was a tyrant who apparently abused his authority. The actual events of his overthrow and the establishment of the Roman Republic that followed are not well understood. On the one hand, it seems certain that, as Livy and other later Roman historians claim, the leading patricians (perhaps led by the legendary heroic patriot Lucius Junius Brutus) had a major hand in ousting him. However, an Etruscan king—Lars Porsenna, of the city of Clusium (about eighty miles northeast of Rome)—may have played a pivotal role. Sometime between 509 and 504 B.C., the period in which modern scholars believe the Republic was established, Porsenna marched his army on Rome. The famous story of Horatius at the bridge (in which a heroic Roman single-handedly holds off the invaders and saves the city from capture) is likely fictitious, or at least exaggerated, for Porsenna did manage to capture the city.

One possible scenario is that Porsenna had agreed to help the Roman fathers get rid of Tarquin (in exchange for some favor or other compensation) but then turned on them and occupied the city. Recent archaeological finds showing that several of Rome's important public buildings burned down about this time may be evidence of a violent takeover. In any case, once Porsenna had taken Rome, he used it as a base to attack other Latin cities to the south. The Latins soon banded together and defeated his army, however, forcing him to retreat homeward and leaving the Romans free to form a new kind of government.

## A People with a Greater Destiny?

That government, the Republic, was run by representatives of the people, although at first Roman leaders defined "the people" rather narrowly. Only free adult males who owned weapons (and were therefore eligible for military service), a group that made up a minority of the population, could vote or hold public office. Some of these citizens met periodically in the Assembly, which now had more power than it had during the Monarchy. They proposed and voted on new laws and also annually elected two consuls, or administrator-generals, to run the state on a day-to-day basis and to lead the army. In his *Laws*, Cicero later described these leaders, as well as the special office of dictator, to be filled in a national emergency:

> There shall be two magistrates with royal powers. . . . They shall be called consuls. In the field they shall hold the supreme military power and shall be subject to no one. The safety of the people shall be their highest law. . . . But when a serious war or civil dissentions arise, one man shall hold, for not longer than six months, the power which ordinarily belongs to the two consuls. . . . And after being appointed under favorable auspices, he shall be master of the people.[24]

The other legislative body, the Senate, was composed exclusively of patricians, who held their positions for life. Although in theory the senators were mere governmental advisers, in reality they usually dictated the policies of the consuls and, through the use of wealth and high position, indirectly influenced the way the members of the Assembly voted. Thus, except under extreme circumstances, the Senate held the real power in republican Rome and the state was an oligarchy (a government run by a select group) rather than a true democracy.

Still, in an age when kings and other absolute monarchs ruled almost everywhere else in the known world, the Roman Republic was a very progressive and enlightened political entity indeed. Though most Romans

# BRAVE HORATIUS DEFENDS THE BRIDGE

This is part of Livy's account (from *Livy: The Early History of Rome*) of Horatius's heroic, although likely mythical, defense of a crucial bridge across the Tiber during the assault launched on Rome by Etruscan king Lars Porsenna.

"On the approach of the Etruscan army, the Romans abandoned their farmsteads and moved into the city. . . . The most vulnerable point [in the defenses] was the wooden bridge, and the Etruscans would have crossed it and forced an entrance into the city, had it not been for the courage of one man, Horatius Cocles—that great soldier whom the fortune of Rome gave to be her shield on that day of peril. . . . The enemy forces came pouring down the hill, while the Roman troops, throwing away their weapons, were behaving more like undisciplined rabble than a fighting force. Horatius acted promptly. . . . Urging [his comrades] . . . to destroy the bridge by fire or steel or any means they could muster, he offered to hold up the Etruscan advance . . . alone. Proudly he took his stand at the outer edge of the bridge. . . . The advancing enemy paused in sheer astonishment at such reckless courage. . . . With defiance in his eyes Horatius confronted the [enemy], challenging one after the other to single combat. . . . For a while they hung back, each waiting for his neighbor to make the first move until shame . . . drove them to action, and with a fierce cry they hurled their spears at the solitary figure who barred their way. Horatius caught the missiles on his shield and, resolute as ever, straddled the bridge and held his ground. The Etruscans moved forward . . . but their advance was suddenly checked by the crash of the falling bridge. . . . [They] could only stare in bewilderment as Horatius . . . plunged fully armed into the water and swam, through the missiles which fell thick around him, safely to the other side, where his friends were waiting to receive him."

*In the Roman Senate, the great Cicero (standing at left) denounces Cataline (sitting at lower right), a disgruntled nobleman who had hatched a plot to topple the government.*

did not have a say in state policy, many had a measurable voice in choosing leaders and making laws. And these laws often offered to members of all classes an umbrella of protection against the arbitrary abuses of potentially corrupt leaders. "Law is the bond which secures these our privileges in the commonwealth [empire]," Cicero later wrote, "the foundation of our . . . liberty, the fountainhead [main source] of justice. Within the law are reposed the mind and heart, the judgment and conviction of the state."[25] For these and other reasons, republican government proved increasingly flexible and largely met the needs of Romans of all classes.

The result was that the Roman people came to view their system with great pride and patriotism. In time they came to believe

that the rise of that system, and indeed the very founding of Rome centuries earlier, was not a chance event; rather, the gods had blessed these national beginnings and ordained that the Romans, the master race, were destined to rule over others. This belief in a greater destiny fueled new and greater stages of Roman expansion, and in the late fifth century B.C. Roman armies began marching outward from Latium. They captured the main Etruscan stronghold of Veii in about 396 B.C., and in the decades that followed, many other towns and peoples of central Italy became incorporated into the growing Roman sphere. By the early third century B.C., after Rome's defeat of the Samnites, a powerful and much-feared hill people, Roman territory had expanded to cover some fifty thousand square miles, well more than a hundred times its original size.

## Conquests Beyond Italy

One important factor in the success of these early conquests was Rome's establishment of "colonies," small towns that served as advanced bases for consolidating recent territorial gains. These colonies were very practical and functional in their layout and demonstrated the Romans' unusual efficiency and practicality. One such base, Alba Fucens (sixty-eight miles east of Rome), set up in 303 B.C. near the end of Rome's second war with the Samnites, was first excavated in 1949. The colony, says noted scholar Paul MacKendrick,

> assured Rome's communications on the two sides of Samnium [a region of the central Apennines], eastward . . .

## BUILDING A ROMAN ARMY CAMP

Rome's success was partly attributable to the high quality of its army, which developed systematic and efficient campaigning and fighting methods and maintained them for centuries. The well-fortified camp constructed daily by a Roman army on the march is just one of many examples. This account of the building of such a camp is from the *Jewish War* of the first-century-A.D. Jewish historian Josephus.

"Whenever they [the Romans] invade hostile territory they rigidly refuse battle till they have fortified their camp. This they do not construct haphazardly or unevenly, nor do they tackle the job . . . without organized squads; if the ground is uneven it is thoroughly leveled, then the site is marked out as a rectangle. To this end, the army is followed by a large number of engineers with all the tools needed for building. The inside is divided up, ready for the huts. From outside, the perimeter looks like a wall and is equipped with towers evenly spaced. In the gaps between the towers they mount [mechanical] spear-throwers, catapults, stone-throwers . . . all ready to be discharged. Four gates are constructed, one in each length of wall, practicable for the entry of baggage-animals and wide enough for armed sorties [detachments of combat troops], if called for. The camp is divided up by streets, accurately marked out; in the middle are erected the officers' huts, and in the middle of these the commander's headquarters, which resembles a shrine. It all seems like a mushroom town, with marketplace, workman's quarters, and orderly-rooms."

and southeastward. . . . Excavating Alba's civic center, [archaeologists] found a forum, with altar and miniature temple, buried under many feet of earth. They also found a basilica (a rectangular roofed hall . . . used as a law court and commercial center). . . . Beside the basilica [was] a market, with baths on one side and a temple on the other. . . . An adjoining street . . . was lined with shops. . . . Walls, grid, civic center, public buildings: these made Alba a smaller and more orderly replica of Rome. The general layout is repeated so often in so many places that it suggests a master plan made in the [office of the] censors [officials in charge of new construction and awarding government contracts] in Rome.[26]

Another key to the Romans' successful early expansion was their gift for political conciliation and organization. Instead of treating former enemies harshly, they opted for the wiser and more fruitful approach of making treaties with them and granting them Roman citizenship and legal privileges. They also initiated the habit of introducing the Latin language, as well as Roman ideas, laws, and customs, to non-Latin peoples, in a sense "Romanizing" them. "What made the Romans so remarkable," comments noted classical scholar Michael Grant,

> was a talent for patient political reasonableness that was unique in the ancient world. . . . On the whole, Rome found it advisable. . . to keep its bargains with its allies, displaying a self-restraint, a readiness to compromise,

and a calculated generosity that the world had never seen. And so the allies, too, had little temptation to feel misused.[27]

However politically astute and reasonable the Romans may have been, the conquest of central Italy did not satisfy their growing appetite for territory and power. In the late 280s B.C., they turned on the numerous Greek cities that had sprung up across southern Italy in the preceding few centuries and in the space of only two decades absorbed them, becoming the undisputed masters of all Italy south of the Po Valley (the northern region at the foot of the Alps). Next, Rome cast its gaze beyond the shores of Italy and onto neighboring Mediterranean coasts. The empire of Carthage (centered in what is now Tunisia, in north Africa) fell to Roman steel after the three devastating Punic Wars, fought between 264 and 146 B.C.[28] As prizes, Rome gained the large and fertile island of Sicily, at the foot of the Italian boot; other western Mediterranean islands; Spain; and much of north Africa.

Rome had originally been strictly a land power; however, out of necessity during the Punic conflicts, it built a powerful navy. Soon after obliterating Carthage, it unleashed its formidable combined land and naval forces on the Greek kingdoms clustered in the Mediterranean's eastern sphere, including Macedonia, Seleucia, and Egypt. By the end of the second century B.C., the Mediterranean had become, in effect, a Roman lake; in fact, thereafter the Romans sometimes rather arrogantly referred to that waterway as *mare nostrum,* "our sea."

## The Fall of the Republic

But Rome's phenomenal success had come at a price. By the dawn of the first century B.C., ominous cracks had appeared in the Republic's structure. First, in their rise to Mediterranean mastery, the Romans had found it increasingly difficult to administer so many diverse lands and peoples with a governmental system that had been designed to rule a single people inhabiting a small city-state. In addition, conquest and rule required large, well-disciplined armies and able generals, both of which, of course, Rome had in abundance. But the state's policy, an unwise one it turned out, did not reward its soldiers with pensions and land when they retired. Meeting this need, the wealthiest and most powerful generals began using their influence to secure such benefits

The Romans lay siege to Carthage in 149 B.C. at the climax of the Third Punic War.

for their men. Consequently, the troops began to show more allegiance to their generals than to the state. They served these leaders, the second-century-A.D. Greek historian Appian wrote,

> not under the compulsion of law, but by private inducements. Nor did they fight against enemies of the state, but against private enemies, nor against foreigners, but against Romans who were their equals in status. All these factors undermined their fear of military discipline. They felt they were not so much serving in the army as lending assistance . . . by their own choice . . . [to leaders who needed them] to attain their private ends.[29]

The "private ends" of these generals increasingly consisted of amassing great political power and challenging the government's authority. Among the most successful were Cornelius Sulla, the first Roman consul to seize the capital by force; Gnaeus Pompey, who won lasting fame after ridding the Mediterranean of pirates; Julius Caesar, who conquered the wild lands of Gaul and met a violent end at the hands of senatorial assassins in 44 B.C.; and Mark Antony, Caesar's protégé, famous for his love affair and alliance with Egypt's queen Cleopatra. These and other contenders for state power met head-on in a series of horrendously destructive civil wars that killed hundreds of thousands of people and brought the Republic and its ideals of representative government crashing down. Cicero, the last great republican champion, quite literally lost his head, the victim of Antony's henchmen.

From this long and destructive orgy of personal ambition and civil strife, one man

*In this famous modern painting, three servants bear the body of Julius Caesar, who has just been as-sassinated by a group of senators who believed he had become a tyrant.*

finally emerged victorious—Octavian, Cae-sar's adopted son. Soon after the defeat of his last rivals, Antony and Cleopatra, in a large naval battle near the Greek town of Actium in 31 B.C., the Senate, now virtually powerless, conferred on Octavian the title of Augustus, "the exalted one." Though quite prudently he never personally used the title of emperor, he became in fact the first ruler of a new, more autocratic Roman state. Des-tined to last even longer than the now de-funct Republic, this vast and powerful realm would become known as the Roman Em-pire.

# THE BLESSINGS OF PEACE AND PLENTY: ROME REACHES ITS ZENITH

During the Roman Empire's first two centuries, the Mediterranean world, almost all of which Rome administered, enjoyed a degree of peace and prosperity it had never known before and would not know again for almost two thousand years. This extraordinary era later became known as the *Pax Romana*, or "Roman peace." Augustus (formerly Octavian) laid its foundation in his forty-two-year reign, which came to be called the Augustan Age, during which he built a firm and lasting foundation for a strong and peaceful country. Among other things, he reorganized the army; created a police force for the city of Rome; reformed both the administration of the provinces and the tax system; built dozens of temples, theaters, and other public buildings; and championed the arts and literature. Indeed, his reign proved to be Rome's greatest artistic and literary golden age. In 1863, an Italian excavator discovered a large statue of Augustus (which has become known as the "Prima Porta Augustus") in Rome. In perfect condition, the sculpture shows him wearing a magnificent breastplate and raising his right arm in a gesture of serene majesty, a fitting symbol of the proud and splendid age he oversaw.

*This magnificent statue of Augustus, the first emperor, was found at Prima Porta, near Rome.*

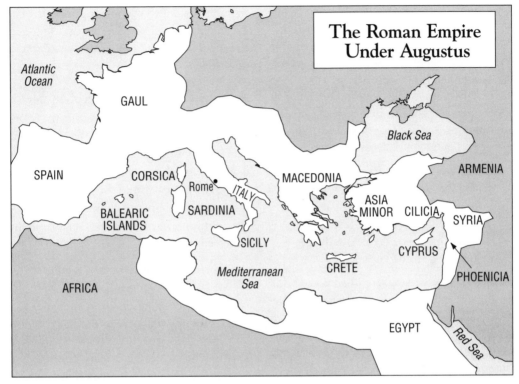

The *Pax Romana* was also the era in which Roman civilization attained its greatest size and political influence. Most of Augustus's immediate successors were thoughtful, effective rulers who brought peace and economic stability to the Roman world.[30] And the five emperors who ruled from 96 to 180—Nerva, Trajan, Hadrian, Antoninus Pius, and Marcus Aurelius—were so capable and enlightened that history later accorded them the collective title of the "five good emperors." They brought the Roman realm to its political, economic, and cultural zenith, prompting the noted eighteenth-century English historian Edward Gibbon to remark,

> If a man were called upon to fix the period in the history of the world during which the condition of the human race was most happy and

prosperous, he would without hesitation name that which elapsed from the accession of Nerva to the death of Aurelius. . . . Their united reigns are possibly the only period of history in which the happiness of a great people was the sole object of government.[31]

## Longings for Peace and Harmony

In many ways, the Empire owed its success and longevity to the shrewdness, determination, and dedicated hard work of its first and greatest ruler, Augustus. Once Augustus had eliminated his adversaries in the Republic's final civil conflict, he confronted the task of reshaping the Roman government as a one-man dictatorship, an act he must have realized would change the face of the Mediterranean world forever. This act also made him the most powerful human being who had ever lived. No doubt sobered by these thoughts, he must have felt more confident when, in August 29 B.C., he heard a private reading of the *Georgics*, poems that his friend Virgil had recently written. The first poem contained a beautiful prayer that beseeched the gods to preserve the health and life of the man who promised to bring peace and order at last to a war-weary world.

> Gods of our fathers, native gods, Romulus and our mother Vesta, you who guard the Tuscan Tiber [River] and the Palatine [hill] of Rome, at least do not prevent this young man from the rescue of an age turned upside down.[32]

With this little prayer, Virgil had voiced the feelings of most of his fellow Romans. The Roman Republic was dead, and memories of its failures and the turbulent, bloody events of its last decades stirred little more than emotional pain and distress in the average Roman. Sick of the seemingly endless civil discords and all the suffering and devastation these had brought, they longed for peace and harmony and believed that "this young man," as Virgil put it, was the one fated to bring about a more tranquil and constructive age.

With the prayers and backing of a majority of the citizens, therefore, Augustus steadily and shrewdly consolidated a wide array of powers, always making sure to do so legally, in accordance with Roman tradition and established law. Through this continuous process of acquiring legal titles, honors, and powers, wrote the second-century Roman historian Dio Cassius, "the power both of the people and of the Senate was wholly transferred into the hands of Augustus."[33] Yet despite the enormous power he now possessed, the new ruler cultivated the image of

a simple man of the people; he and his wife, Livia, lived in a modest house and shunned the usual lavish lifestyle of the wealthy and powerful.

## A New City of Polished Marble

The new look Rome acquired in the years that followed was anything but modest, however. It was during Augustus's reign that Rome, long a dingy, graceless, and unattractive city, at last became the grand metropolis of polished marble that awed the world in the centuries that followed. "Augustus built a new Forum," says Chester Starr,

> which had its center in a temple of Mars the Avenger [god of war]; around the edge of his Forum were statues of great heroes of Rome, including his own ancestors. In addition, he erected so many theaters, porticoes [column-lined porches and walkways], and other buildings that Rome began to be a truly great city.[34]

Most of these once-splendid structures have since disappeared or fallen into ruin. But archaeologists are able to deduce what many of them originally looked like using a combination of methods. First, they study the remains of foundations, pillars, and other structural components, as well as sculptures and other decorative elements that have survived. Those buildings and their parts that still lie below ground are carefully unearthed, then photographed while still lying in their original positions (*in situ*), partly to give scholars an accurate picture of how the site's individual elements are related to one another. For example, artifacts found in deeper layers are usually (though not always) older than those found above them. Eventu-

*The remains of the Temple of Mars Ultor (the "Avenger"), in the Forum of Augustus, which Augustus himself dedicated in 2 B.C. This forum also featured bronze statues of important Roman generals.*

ally, excavators remove the more delicate artifacts and take them to museums for preservation and study.

On occasion, archaeologists find enough of a structure's original parts to attempt a full reconstruction. This was the fortunate case with the crowning artistic masterpiece of the Augustan Age, the *Ara Pacis* ("Altar of Peace"), completed in 9 B.C. As Paul MacKendrick explains,

> The reconstructed Altar of Peace . . . must be recognized as one of the great triumphs of Italian archaeology. Sculptured reliefs from this structure were

first discovered, though not recognized as such, as long ago as 1568. . . . The reliefs were first recognized as belonging to the altar in 1879. But it was not until 1937–38 that [archaeologists] carried through the incredibly ingenious and patient work which led to the almost complete recovery and reconstruction of the altar. . . . The altar itself, in the center of its enclosed platform, proved to be U-shaped, with the open end of the U facing west . . . and approached by a flight of steps. The whole was fenced off by a marble wall about thirty feet square and six-teen feet high, with wide doorways on the east and west . . . . Each face of the enclosure wall bore two wide hor-izontal decorative bands. . . . On the outer face the wide upper band bore a frieze [band of sculptures] with over 100 figures.[35]

Among the figures represented in the frieze are Augustus himself and members of his family.

Another way that excavators can tell how ancient Roman structures originally looked is by examining images of such buildings in surviving wall and vase paintings. In this re-gard, ancient coins are especially helpful. "Religion," writes Michael Grant,

as well as other considerations, prompted the Roman authorities to depict tem-ples on their coinage, and these repre-sentations have added to our knowledge of the appearance and structure of such buildings, as well as the works of art they contained. . . . This is information that either supplements the literary sources or reveals structures of which those sources (and excavations) tell us nothing.[36]

## Augustan Literature

Augustus, a master of political propaganda, did not pass up the chance to take credit for his massive building programs. In the *Res*

*Pictured here is one of the beautiful friezes (carved panels) decorating the walls of Augustus's Altar of Peace. Augustus and the members of his family were also depicted on the monument.*

## THE BLESSINGS OF PEACE

Augustan poet Albius Tibullus (ca. 54–19 B.C.) was an avowed pacifist, which made him a rarity among Roman men. The elegies he produced in his short career were filled with references to peace, love, and pastoral simplicity—major literary themes of the Augustan Age—as evidenced in this excerpt (translated by James Cranstoun in Godolphin's *The Latin Poets*) that lists the many blessings of peace.

Who was the man who first forged the fatal blade?
Oh! cruel he [was] and of an iron soul!
Then war and carnage first made gory raid,
Opening a shorter way to life's dreary goal [death]. . . .

Peace dwell with us! fair Peace and nothing else before
Yoked the curved plow to the sturdy steer [ox];
Peace reared the vine [and] with vine-juice filled the store [storage bins]
With which the sire [father] his loving son might cheer. . . .

Let savage warriors wield the sword and spear,
But keep aloof [away] from the gentle damsel's door;
Come bounteous Peace! still hold the wheaten ear [crops],
And from your joyous lap rich fruits outpour.

*gestae*, the brief summary he left of his own achievements, he boasted:

I repaired the Capitol [the Capitoline hill, on which rested temples of Jupiter] and the theater of Pompey with enormous expenditures [of money] on both works, without having my name inscribed on them. I repaired the conduits of the aqueducts [stone structures that piped water] which were falling into ruin in many places. . . . I completed the Julian Forum and the basilica which was between the temple of Castor and the temple of Saturn, works begun . . . by my father [his adoptive father, Julius Caesar].[37]

Augustus also bragged about the great sums he spent to stage public entertainment, such as gladiator fights, and to replenish the state treasury during hard times, all from his own pockets.

An equally impressive Augustan achievement was the fine flowering of literature in this period. With his keen sense of the power of propaganda, Augustus realized that the written word was a powerful tool he could use to promote his various programs and to emphasize Rome's mission to bring order to the

# LOVE AT THE RACETRACK

The love poems of the Augustan poet Ovid (43 B.C.–A.D. 17) were witty, usually lighthearted and charming, and often sexually frank. The latter fact got him in trouble with the somewhat prudish Augustus, who eventually banished the writer to a remote town on the coast of the Black Sea. In this excerpt from Ovid's *Art of Love* (quoted in Shelton's *As the Romans Did*), he openly advocates flirting with women at the racetrack.

"Don't neglect the horse races if you're looking for a place to meet your girlfriend. A circus [racetrack] crowded with people offers many advantages. You don't have to use a secret sign language here. . . . Sit right next to your girlfriend—no one will stop you—and squeeze up beside her as closely as possible. . . . The narrowness of each seating space forces you to squeeze together; in fact the rules for seating compel you to touch her! Conversation should begin with no problem; just start out with the same comments that everyone else is making. Be sure to ask with great interest which horses are running and then immediately cheer for the same one, whichever it is, that she cheers for. Perhaps a speck of dust will settle on your girlfriend's breast (it often happens); be sure to brush it off with your hand. Even if there is no speck of dust, pretend—and keep brushing off nothing! Take advantage of every opportunity. . . . In addition, turn to whoever is sitting behind her and ask him not to jab her in the back with his knees. These little touches win over simple female hearts. . . . It's also helpful to fan her with the racing program and to give her a stool for her dainty feet. Yes, the circus provides many opportunities for initiating a love affair."

*A later European rendering of the Augustan poet Ovid shows him wearing a crown of leaves.*

whole world. This motive, coupled with his genuine love of literature and ideas, led him to encourage thinkers and writers. "Augustus gave all possible encouragement to intellectuals," the first-century-A.D. Roman historian Suetonius wrote. "He would politely and impatiently attend readings not only of their poems and historical works, but of their speeches and dialogues."[38]

Writers in Augustan Rome, however, received much more than just moral and verbal support. At Augustus's urging, many of his wealthy friends patronized (provided complete financial support for) writers and artists, allowing them to create at their leisure without having to worry about making a living. The emperor's close associate Gaius Maecenas became the greatest literary patron of the age. Most of Rome's best-known and beloved writers, including the poets Virgil, Horace, and Propertius, became part of Maecenas's elite literary circle. The poet Ovid, master of the love letter and love elegy (a series of verses describing a poet's changing relationship with a woman), had a different patron, and Livy, the great Augustan historian, received encouragement from Augustus himself. The result of so many talented individuals receiving such generous support from society's highest levels was a literary outpouring greater in scope and quality than Rome had ever produced before or would ever produce again. (The Augustan Age of literature is usually dated from the death of the last great republican writer, Cicero, in 43 B.C., to the death of the Augustan poet Ovid in A.D. 17.)

The works of the Augustan writers had a profound and lasting impact, not only on later Roman society but also on the literature and philosophy of later medieval and modern Europe. This was partly because they ably captured the sincere feelings of re-lief, joy, optimism, and renewal that permeated their times, making their works extremely vigorous and passionate. They also labored diligently over every word, phrase, and line, striving, like none before them, to achieve the most perfect and beautiful forms possible. In doing so, they took full advantage of the exceptional qualities of the Latin language. In fact, Michael Grant states, Latin gave these works considerable originality because it "proved able to create both resonant [full and pleasing], vigorously compact prose and poetry of stirringly profound, harmonious musicality."[39] Many of the finest of Europe's later writers greatly admired and tried to imitate the preciseness and overall beauty of Augustan literature.

Perhaps the most beloved of all the Augustan writers, both in his own time and in later ages, was Virgil, author of the stately *Aeneid*. This work, seen as Rome's national epic, not only told the stirring story of Aeneas, the Trojan prince whose family lineage supposedly gave rise to the Romans, but also prophesied that Roman civilization would continue forever. It is not difficult to understand why such plots and themes appealed so much to the Romans of Virgil's day. He put into stirring words and verses the Romans' deep pride in their past and their belief that they had a superior destiny. Summing up Virgil's appeal to his countrymen, R. H. Barrow writes,

> The most significant movement of history . . . according to Virgil, is the march of the Roman along the road of his destiny to a high civilization; for in that destiny is to be found the valid and permanent interpretation of all [human] movement and all development. . . . The stately *Aeneid* progresses

*A young Roman woman has fainted, supposedly overcome by the beauty of Virgil's verses. Virgil is universally recognized as Rome's greatest epic poet.*

throughout its length to this theme, the universal and the ultimate triumph of the Roman spirit as the highest manifestation of man's powers.[40]

## A Fateful Turning Point

Despite its long list of positive achievements, the Augustan Age had a darker side, one that would have negative consequences for Rome's future. Throughout most of the years of the Republic, Rome's overall military strategy had been largely offensive, stimulating a steady expansion of the realm. The usual scenario was for the Romans to defeat a people, consolidate their territory, and then Romanize and absorb them, thereby expanding Roman frontiers. Although no one suspected it at the time, the fateful turning

point that marked the start of the transition to a *defensive* military posture, and thereby planted the seeds of long-term Roman military decline, came in A.D. 9, late in Augustus's reign.

When Augustus had come to power, the Empire's northern border was a ragged, ill-defined frontier that ran west to east through south-central Europe. Over the centuries, the Germanic tribes who inhabited the regions north of that border had periodically pressed southward, threatening Roman territory. An invasion of two warlike tribes, the Cimbri and Teutones, whom the Roman general Gaius Marius defeated in 102 B.C., was a prominent example. Like other Roman leaders, Augustus felt that the Germans' close proximity to the Roman heartland was dangerous and intolerable. So he set about pushing the northern borders back. Beginning in the mid-20s B.C., his armies slowly advanced northward, establishing new towns in the areas they secured.

These campaigns increased in size and speed. And after several years of intermittent fighting, Roman territory extended to the Danube River, prompting the creation of some new provinces. The frontier then remained relatively quiet for a few years, until Augustus sent an official named Publius Quinctilius Varus to turn a section of Germany into still another new province. In A.D. 9, in the dense Teutoburg Forest (some eighty miles east of the Rhine River), a large force of Germans ambushed Varus and his three legions (about fifteen thousand troops in all), killing them almost to the last man. According to Suetonius, Augustus "took the disaster so deeply to heart that he left his hair and beard untrimmed for months; he would often beat his head on a door, shouting: 'Quinctilius Varus, give me back my legions!'"[41] Varus could not give the legions back, of course. And the fact was that no one, including Augustus, could replace them. Raising, outfitting, and training three entire legions was too expensive a proposition, even for someone as wealthy as the emperor.

More ominously, in the years immediately following Varus's defeat, the Romans became discouraged, wrote off Germany as a loss, and pulled their forces back, allowing the natives to maintain control of the area. The result was that Germany was not absorbed into the Empire and thoroughly Romanized, as other parts of Europe had been. Permanently retaining their independence, the northern tribes (whom the Romans called "barbar-

ians") proved an increasingly dangerous threat in later times, especially in Rome's last two centuries. In view of their final triumph over Rome, the encounter in the Teutoburg Forest ranks as one of the most crucial and decisive battles in world history.

Since neither Augustus, nor any of his subjects, nor any of his immediate successors and their subjects could foresee these long-range developments, the Romans looked on Augustus's reign as a glorious high-water mark in their saga. He was hailed as "the father of his country" (by the citizenry) and even as "the son of god" (by Virgil and other writers). And when he died on August 19, A.D. 14, at the age of seventy-six, millions deeply mourned and many wept openly.

*Facing the shame of total defeat at the hands of the barbarians, Varus takes his own life.*

45

## DISASTER IN A GERMAN FOREST

In this excerpt from his *Roman History* (Ian Scott-Kilvert's translation), Dio Cassius describes the last hours of the ill-fated Roman army under the command of P. Quinctilius Varus in Germany's dense Teutoburg Forest.

"A violent downpour and storm developed, so that the column [of soldiers] was strung out [over a distance]; this also caused the ground around the tree-roots . . . to become slippery, making movement very dangerous. . . . While the Romans were struggling against the elements, the barbarians suddenly surrounded them on all sides at once, stealing through the densest thickets, as they were familiar with the paths. At first they hurled their spears from a distance . . . [and then] closed in to shorter range; for their own part the Roman troops . . . were everywhere overwhelmed by their opponents [and] suffered many casualties and were quite unable to counter-attack. . . . They could neither draw their bows nor hurl their javelins to any effect, nor even make use of their shields, which were completely sodden with rain. . . . Besides this the enemy's numbers had been greatly reinforced . . . [making] it easier to encircle and strike down the Romans, whose ranks . . . had lost many men. . . . So every soldier and every horse was cut down."

## The Accomplishments of Augustus's Successors

For the most part, Augustus's immediate successors maintained the peace his reign had initiated. There were occasional violent episodes, to be sure. In 43, for instance, the emperor Claudius (reigned 41–54) launched a full-scale invasion of Britain (a task that Julius Caesar had begun but not completed in the previous century), and much of that island soon became a new Roman province. After a huge fire destroyed large sections of the capital city in 64, the emperor Nero (51–68) unfairly blamed the disaster on members of a relatively new and still small religious sect, the Christians; this marked the first of many Christian persecutions that

would occur in the following two centuries. Then, in 69, soon after the corrupt Nero had been branded an enemy of the people by the Senate (which still retained much prestige, if little power) and committed suicide, a violent power struggle erupted. Because four different army generals claimed the throne, that year became known as "the year of the four emperors." The winner of the struggle was Vespasian (69–79), who launched a new dynasty (ruling family), the Flavians, and with his son Titus (79–81) successfully and severely crushed a major Jewish rebellion in the province of Judaea in Palestine.

These exceptional turbulent episodes aside, the rulers of the *Pax Romana* carried out numerous positive and constructive programs.

Claudius built many fine roads, aqueducts, and temples and significantly expanded the civil service in the Empire's provinces. Vespasian was also a great builder. According to Suetonius,

> In Rome, which had been made unsightly by fires and collapsed buildings, Vespasian authorized anyone who pleased to take over the vacant sites, and build on them if the original owners failed to come forward. He personally inaugurated the restoration of the burned Capitol, by collecting the first basketfull of rubble and carrying it away on his shoulders. . . . He also started work on several new buildings: a temple of Peace near the Forum, [and] a temple to Claudius . . . on the Caelian hill . . . [a structure] almost completely destroyed by Nero.[42]

The greatest such achievement of Vespasian and his dynasty was the Colosseum. Completed in the heart of Rome in 81, it was an immense amphitheater (seating up to fifty thousand people) for staging gladiatorial combats and wild animal shows. The study, protection, and partial restoration of this most famous of all Roman monuments have proved to be one of the largest archaeological challenges of modern times. In 1825, workmen set up massive stone buttresses to help keep the surviving sections of the façade from collapsing, and in 1870 all of the vegetation, which had long choked the structure's interior, was cleared. Major restoration efforts occurred from 1893 to 1896, in 1933, and in the mid- to late 1970s.

Then, in 1992, the largest such restoration project ever attempted began. Estimated to take ten to fifteen years to complete, the project's minimum goals were to repair and clean existing intact surfaces and to replace the arena floor, which archaeologists removed in the 1800s. One very costly and difficult goal was to move Rome's Metro B subway tunnel, which ran beneath the Colosseum, to a lower position, because of concern that the vibrations from passing trains might cause the structure to weaken and further deteriorate. This is only one example of how archaeologists attempting to excavate and preserve ancient Roman structures have to deal with, and are sometimes severely impeded by, the presence of modern construction.

*The infamous emperor Nero, who, among other outrages, killed his own wife and mother.*

## Roman Grandeur, System, and Order

Even in ruin, the Colosseum remains a grand symbol of Rome's past. In a like manner, when it was newly built it symbolized the grandeur of Rome's present, as the Empire approached its height of power and supremacy. Under the emperor Trajan (98–117), that realm was larger than it ever had been or ever would be. It stretched from the Atlantic Ocean in the west to the Persian Gulf in the east, and from northern Africa in the south to central Britain in the north, a colossal political unit encompassing some 3.5 million square miles and some 100 million people.

Yet it was not just its size that made the Empire great in these years. Consistently effective and uncommonly humane leadership made it a safe, prosperous, and pleasant place to live for most of its inhabitants. Trajan, for instance, devoted almost all of his energies to running a fair and efficient government. And his immediate successors did the same. Hadrian (117–138) expanded the Roman welfare system, created free schools for poor children, and strengthened laws protecting slaves from abuse. And his successor, Antoninus Pius, was so ethical, honest, and sincere that his first official act as emperor was to donate his large personal fortune to the

*The remains of the splendid Colosseum readily attest that the Romans were the greatest builders of the ancient world.*

public treasury. Thus, when Marcus Aurelius (161–180) took the throne on Antoninus's passing in 161, their contemporary, the Greek writer Aelius Aristides, hardly exaggerated in his praise of the Roman achievement:

> Every place is full of gymnasia, fountains, gateways, temples, shops, and schools. . . . Only those outside your Empire, if there are any, are fit to be pitied for losing such blessings. . . . You have surveyed the whole world . . . and civilized it all with system and order.[43]

Unbeknownst to the new emperor and his largely happy subjects, however, Rome's great era of peace and plenty was about to end. The specters of war, disease, political instability, economic decline, and social unrest were massing for a combined assault, the effects of which would reach a ruinous crescendo in the coming century. Aurelius was as hardworking, just, and honest a ruler as has ever lived. But he had no power to stop, nor was he likely even aware of, the mass migrations of Germanic tribes through northern Europe that would soon send barbarian hordes spilling over Roman borders. Nor can he be held responsible for the in-

*A bust depicts Marcus Aurelius, a man of high principle and the last of the so-called good emperors.*

competence, greed, dishonesty, and brutality of his successors. In the years following his passing, for the first time in living memory, large numbers of Romans began to accept the formerly inconceivable idea that Rome might not be invincible. And they were afraid.

# STRIVING TO MAINTAIN TRADITION: ROMAN SOCIAL CLASSES AND INSTITUTIONS

Roman society was never static; rather, it was always growing and changing as the Roman state, its institutions, and its citizenry reacted to changing times, needs, and opportunities. As in modern societies, views about what Roman society deemed moral, proper, and worthwhile evolved over the course of the centuries. In Rome's earliest days, for example, most people, even those few who were well-to-do, generally lived simple, austere lives and looked on unnecessary luxury as improper and a potentially corrupting influence. Besides horse races, there were few public games. This was because the authorities, striving to maintain conservative traditional values, thought that such displays promoted public laziness or posed a threat to public order. In the late Republic and early Empire, however, many such conservative attitudes relaxed, partly because of Rome's contact with other peoples, especially the more liberal Greeks. Amassing great wealth and luxury became more acceptable to many Romans, and public games of all kinds became widely popular throughout the Roman world.

Still, these and many other outward changes did not alter the Romans' reverence for and desire to uphold basic traditions. Certain Roman institutions long maintained their traditional structure and rules, or at least their prestige, even when they grew with the times. The family, presided over by its male head, for instance, remained the cornerstone of society throughout Rome's long history. Scholars know a good deal about how a Roman family and its household worked, partly because of surviving written sources, especially personal letters, and also through archaeological finds, including the remains of townhouses and villas and tomb epitaphs and other inscriptions.

Another traditional institution that remained a fundamental reality of Roman life through the ages was the patronage system, in which people of lower social rank did favors for those with higher rank and prestige. People also counted on government to provide a measure of stability in their lives. Although its outer trappings changed on occasion (from the Republic to the Empire, for example), Roman government nearly always supported certain basic principles and traditional, time-honored customs, beliefs, and institutions. These included religious practices and festivals, the prestige and moral authority of the Senate (even when it came to have no real power), and the regular administration of law and justice. A large body of laws collected over the centuries was, in fact, one of Roman society's great anchors, an institution Romans of all classes felt they could rely on for protection, no matter who was in power. "Rome's monumental achievement," wrote the late, great scholar Edith Hamilton, "was law. A people violent by nature, of enormous appetites and brutal force, produced the great Law of Nations, which sustained with equal justice the rights of free-born men everywhere."[44]

*This nineteenth-century rendering shows a foreign emissary addressing members of the early Roman Senate. Even in the Empire, when the Senate had little real power, its members retained great prestige.*

# WHAT'S IN A NAME?

A discussion of the different kinds of Roman people would be incomplete without considering the names these people used. Roman names had much more profound meaning and importance than those in modern societies do; they denoted social status and family history as well as personal identity. For example, a free Roman male used his nomen, the name of his clan, which often indicated social rank and status. Nomina ending in the suffix -ius, such as Fabius, Julius, and Cornelius, were ancient clan names reserved for patricians. Less prestigious nomina had endings such as -acus, -enus, and -ca.

Roman men also used two other names—the cognomen, denoting the particular extended family within the specified clan, and the praenomen, or first name, identifying the individual himself. The normal order of the three names was praenomen-nomen-cognomen. Thus, the famous military general Gaius Julius Caesar was Gaius, of the Caesar family, of the clan of the Julii. To the frequent frustration of modern historians and students, the normal order of these names was often changed for various reasons, such as poets trying to match the names to rhymes and meter.

Women's names were much less complex at first. In the Republic, most young girls went by a feminine form of the father's nomen, so Gaius Julius Caesar's daughter was called Julia, and Marcus Tullius Cicero's daughter was known as Tullia. Later, however, as women's social status improved, threefold names for women became fairly common, with the same confusing variations in arrangement as in men's names.

The names of slaves and freedmen, except in the early days of the Republic, were no simpler. At first, slaves were called *por*, a slang version of the Latin word *puer*, meaning "boy," and identified with their master's praenomen. Thus, Marcipor was "Marcus's boy," Aulipor was "Aulus's boy," and so forth. Later, however, slaves were given individual names, usually of foreign origin, and also the nomen and praenomen of their masters. Still more confusing were freedmen's names, which consisted of their original slave name, followed by the nomen of the former master, then by a cognomen assigned at will by the master when freeing the person, and finally by the letter *l*, which stood for *libertus*, the Latin word for a freedman. In response to Shakespeare's famous question "What's in a name?" Romans of all walks of life, always conscious of and sensitive about family affiliations and their social status, would undoubtedly answer, "A great deal!"

## Social Classes and Patronage

The fact that Rome evolved from an ancient tribal society, one based principally on the ownership and exploitation of land, profoundly influenced the development of its family and social structure and the status, both public and private, of the various people within that structure. Before and during the dimly remembered era of Romulus, of course, the chief landholders—the *patres*—had emerged as the wealthiest and strongest figures in the community. Each of these Roman fathers headed a separate *gens*, a tribal clan made up of several extended families related by blood. The clan heads constituted the early Roman nobility—the landowning patrician class. Their influence, stemming from their prestige (*dignitas*) and moral authority (*auctoritas*), extended not only over the many members of their individual clans but often also over the state. This was because most of Rome's senators and a good many of its military generals (and later its governors and emperors) came from this privileged, respected, and envied social class.

The patricians were not the only Roman citizens (*cives*) wielding wealth and influence, however. During the Republic, as Rome's empire expanded and became powerful and prosperous, a few businessmen gained great wealth and prominence and formed a non–land-based aristocracy second in prestige only to the patricians. This was the equestrian class (sometimes referred to as the "knights"). As Michael Grant explains, these two groups, representing only a tiny fraction of the population, managed to control society partly because Roman law

was biased in favor of the privileged classes, and . . . their words and per-

sons carried an ill-defined but very real authority, based on the social estimation of their honor and the prestige [of] their position. . . . The ruling groups controlled . . . and exploited the labor which . . . they needed in order to enforce their power. . . . It

*The patrician depicted in this sculpture proudly displays busts of his illustrious ancestors.*

was wealth that gave honor to Rome. Landed wealth was the only truly respectable asset—and the best thing of all was to have inherited it.[45]

The "labor" that the upper classes exploited consisted partly of slaves (who were not citizens) but was also composed of the lower classes of citizens, the plebeians (or plebs), who made up the bulk of the population. Another way the privileged classes controlled the plebs was through the patronage system, in which the heads of well-to-do families became the patrons (*patroni*) of less well-off clients (*clientes*). A patrician patron's dependent plebeian clients usually voted as he directed and supported him in other ways in exchange for his financial and legal protection. In addition, freed slaves were expected to become the clients of their former masters. "The very root of Roman society," Grant adds, "was the institution of a relatively few rich patrons . . . linked with their more numerous poor clients."[46]

Not all clients were lower-class or poor, however, for the patronage system extended throughout the ranks of Roman society. Though a well-to-do aristocrat had many clients of his own, he, in turn, was a client to someone even more wealthy or powerful. The most obvious example was during the Empire, when Rome's highest elite sought and benefited from the emperor's patronage.

## Human Bones Tell a Tale

The differences among the people of these classes—between rich and poor, aristocrat and commoner, and so forth—were purely a matter of social tradition and convention.

Physically, most Romans were of the same racial type (Caucasian, often with swarthy Mediterranean complexions); usually such factors as dress styles, physical bearing, and speech quality and dialects were the only ways to tell them apart. We know what the average Roman (as well as a fair number of specific Romans) looked like partly because of descriptions in ancient writings. More important, numerous statues, busts, and vase and wall paintings depicting Roman people have survived.

Unfortunately, these kinds of relics do not reveal certain kinds of crucial physical information about ancient Roman people, such as their average size, physical and nutritional conditions, kinds and frequency of illness, and life expectancy. To learn about these things, archaeologists need to examine actual human remains. However, finding complete Roman skeletons, scholar Joseph J. Deiss points out, "has proved one of the rarest of archaeological finds, chiefly because the Romans practiced cremation after death."[47]

The most rewarding of these rare finds was the discovery (by Italian archaeologist Giuseppe Maggi in 1980) of more than 150 complete skeletons at Herculaneum. During the eruption of Mt. Vesuvius in A.D. 79, hundreds of the town's residents fled to the waterfront in an attempt to escape by boat. There, blasts of hot gases smothered them to death, and subsequently their bodies were buried and well preserved. Analyses of these remains have revealed the ages of the victims, cavities and abscesses in their teeth, bone scars showing that some performed constant heavy work (and therefore that these were likely slaves), and their nutritional histories. The skeleton of a Roman

*This mummified body of a Roman was preserved by the A.D. 79 eruption of Mount Vesuvius.*

soldier (the only complete such skeleton ever found) was particularly revealing. "He was well nourished," Deiss writes, "strong and tough, and carried carpentry tools. His forearms displayed a heavy muscle build-up, and he had the muscles for bareback riding. He had had a flesh wound in his left thigh, and three of his front teeth had been knocked out."[48] Studies of these skeletons have also shown that the men averaged 5 feet 7 inches in height and the women 5 feet 1 1/2 inches; about 20 percent had suffered some kind of injury or trauma in their lives; and several of them had unusually high levels of lead in their bones (probably from the constant use of lead water pipes and cooking vessels).

## Fathers and Mothers

Twelve of the skeletons found at Herculaneum were huddled together embracing one another at the moment of death, and they appear to have formed a single family group. (Archaeologists have come to call them "the household in flight.") Such a display of familial closeness and cohesiveness is hardly surprising, for supporting the clans, the class structure, the patronage system, and the rest of the framework of Roman society was its most basic and time-honored unit—the family. The Latin word for family, *familia*, translates literally as "household." Many Roman families were nuclear (consisting of a mother, father, and their children) as is common today; although some were extended (typically including a father and mother; unmarried daughters; sons and adopted sons, either unmarried or married and with their own wives, sons, and unmarried daughters; and any uncles, aunts, and/or cousins who, for one reason or another, had no one to support them).

The head of the family was the paterfamilias (plural is patresfamilias), usually the oldest father present. According to ancient tradition, he held absolute power and authority (known as *patria potestas*) over all other members of the household, including of course any slaves or hired workers who lived with the family. In actual practice, however, most Roman family heads were not merciless tyrants. Cases of fathers throwing their wives or children out or killing them were relatively rare and occurred mostly in Rome's earlier centuries. Over time, new laws set certain restrictions on the *patria potestas*, and in any case calls from a father's relatives, friends, and peers asking him to act reasonably tended to restrain a father from unusually cruel behavior. According to scholar Harold Johnston, "Custom, not law, obliged the paterfamilias to call a council of relatives and friends when he contemplated inflicting severe punishment upon his children, and public opinion obliged him to abide by its verdict."[49]

*This portrait bust of a Roman woman dates from sometime between 20 B.C. and A.D. 20.*

By tradition, the materfamilias, the paterfamilias's wife or mother, was also subject to the absolute authority of the male head of household. Though Roman women were considered citizens, like women in other ancient societies they did not enjoy the same rights as male citizens. In the early years of the Republic, Roman men treated their women largely as inferiors, mainly because men saw themselves as more intelligent and competent. As Cicero, writing in the more enlightened and less chauvinistic first century B.C., described it, "Our ancestors established the rule that all women, because of their weakness of intellect, should be under the power of guardians."[50] These guardians were always men, who controlled the property of their wives, mothers, and daughters and barred them from voting, holding public office, or initiating divorce proceedings.

By Cicero's time, the lot of Roman women had improved considerably, and it continued to improve in the first two centuries of the Empire. Women gained the rights to inherit and control their own property and to file for divorce at will, and in most (though certainly not all) households became more men's partners than their servants. A few women even ventured into roles and occupations usually filled only by men. Cases of female doctors, writers, business owners, and even gladiators have been documented. It should be noted, however, that despite their many rights and freedoms, Roman women never gained the rights to vote or hold public office, and the duration and breadth of their educations never compared to those of men. So even in the relatively liberal early years of the Roman Empire, women did not gain complete equality.

## Foreigners, Slaves, and Freedmen

Women were not the only people in the Roman world who were denied equal rights with male *cives*. Foreigners, called *peregrini*, were allowed to do business with Roman citizens but lacked basic rights of citizenship such as voting and serving in the army. The *peregrini*, whose ranks for a long time included provincials, the residents of Rome's many provinces, also had to pay various taxes from which citizens were exempt. Over time, the status of provincials improved markedly. For example, laws evolved providing that if a provincial married a citizen, the former automatically received full citizens' rights. Finally, in A.D. 212, the emperor Caracalla extended full citizenship to all free provincials, and from that time on the term *peregrini* referred only to residents of nations outside Roman-controlled territory.

Slaves, of course, never enjoyed the civil rights of free Romans. During the Republic, most slaves were prisoners captured in wars. During the Empire, when Rome waged few foreign wars, owners replenished their slave ranks by breeding their household slaves or by buying new ones in foreign slave markets. Accurate data concerning the numbers of slaves in the average household or in society in general have not survived. But apparently about five to ten slaves was the minimum for an equestrian or patrician of moderate means; richer individuals owned sixty, seventy, or even hundreds of slaves. (One private owner, Gaius Caelius Isidorus, owned 4,116 slaves!) Historians estimate that in the early years of the Empire slaves made up from one-quarter to one-third of the total population of Italy.

Slavery was a wretched and inhumane institution no matter where or when it existed. Yet it was an accepted fact of life everywhere in the ancient world, condoned and practiced even by freedmen, or former slaves. (The notorious slave owner Isidorus mentioned above was himself a freedman.) And it is noteworthy that the Romans, principally during the Empire, made considerable strides toward making slavery more humane. As scholar Leonardo Dal Maso points out, the lot of Roman slaves "was considerably less unhappy and inhumane than it was among other peoples both

*Slaves are sold on a Roman auction block. Around the neck each wears a* titulus, *a placard listing his or her qualifications and serving as a warranty that the vendor will reimburse the buyer if the slave proves defective.*

## A Love Letter to His Wife

The high degree of love and respect many Roman men came to feel for their wives by late republican and early imperial times is illustrated by this excerpt from a letter (translated by William Melmouth) penned by the first-century-A.D. writer Pliny the Younger to his wife while she was away.

"To Calpurnia: It is incredible how I miss you; such is the tenderness of my affection for you, and so unaccustomed are we to a separation! I lie awake the greatest part of the night in conjuring up your image, and by day . . . my feet carry me of their own accord to your apartment, at those hours I used to visit you; but not finding you there, I return with as much sorrow and disappointment as an excluded lover."

in ancient times and in the medieval and modern periods. Proof of this are the severe laws which protected them and determined their treatment."[51] These laws included, among many others, an edict in the first century A.D. allowing slaves to register complaints of unjust treatment by their masters; a law passed in A.D. 83 forbidding a master from castrating his male slaves; and, finally, in the second century, a law allowing for the prosecution of a master who killed his own slave.[52]

Indeed, many slaves became important, outspoken, trusted, and even loved members of Roman households. Archaeology has revealed tomb inscriptions containing warm and sincere tributes to deceased slaves. Moreover, numerous household slaves received periodic gifts of money or even small but regular wages from their masters. This enabled some slaves to save enough to buy their freedom eventually. Other slaves became freedmen when a kind owner freed them as a gesture of thanks for years of loyal service.

## Various Kinds of Houses

The houses in which Roman fathers, mothers, their children and other relatives, and their slaves lived varied considerably in size, style, and degree of luxury, depending on the wealth and social status of the owners or renters. Even in the late Republic and early Empire, when Rome was most prosperous, most farmers were poor; so they lived in humble dwellings with few comforts, often little more advanced than the eighth-century-B.C. huts archaeologists had excavated on the Palatine. Their poor counterparts in the cities dwelled in crowded one- or two-room rented apartments (cenaculae) packed into large tenement blocks (insulae), often several stories high. From late republican times to the end of the Empire, the vast majority of the capital city's inhabitants lived in such tenements.

Scholars know what these structures looked like because of extensive excavations begun by Italian archaeologist Guido Calza in the 1940s at Ostia, Rome's port town.

Some of the *insulae* uncovered there were nicer than others, featuring large inner courtyards with gardens, walkways, and fountains that all the tenants in the block shared. Even in the better blocks, though, as Paul MacKendrick points out, "there is a certain deadly sameness about these flats where the lower middle class lived out their lives of quiet desperation, as they do in the unfashionable quarters of Rome today."[53]

By contrast, well-to-do Romans resided in more spacious homes—townhouses (*domus*) in the city and villas in the countryside. Not surprisingly, there were always far fewer wealthy townhouses than poor and middle-class apartments. (A surviving fourth-century-A.D. public record lists 46,602 *insulae* in Rome, compared with only 1,797 private *domus*.) Several such townhouses, both large and ornate and smaller and less splendid, have been excavated at another town destroyed by Vesuvius—Pompeii. According to one writer's description, in most of these residences,

> the door from the street opened into a narrow vestibule [passage] that led to [several] wings, open courts, porticoes [porches], small chambers, and corridors. Some sections of the building might incorporate a second story, while other parts stood open to the sky. At the entrance to a typical house lay the atrium, a partially roofed court with a pool to catch rainwater, surrounded by an assortment of smaller rooms.[54]

*A depiction of the atrium (foyer or front hall) of a well-to-do Roman townhouse. Rainwater collected in a cistern on the roof and fell through the opening in the ceiling into the pool below.*

The larger *domus* in Pompeii and other Roman cities also had rooms for the servants and extensive gardens (often with fountains and pools), and they were decorated with beautiful colored mosaic tiles, wall paintings, and bronze and marble statues and busts.

## Government and Law

No matter what kind of home they could afford, all Romans looked to their country's government and laws to provide them with a certain measure of stability and security, mainly in the form of protection and fair treatment. It is not surprising, therefore, that Roman governmental and legal institutions always rested on two principles that the people found reliable and comforting—tradition and continuity.

As forms of government, the Republic and Empire certainly seem, at first glance, to be very different and lacking in continuity. The former was, after all, guided by officials elected by the people (at least in theory), while the latter appeared to operate largely according to the whims of a single man—the emperor. Yet beneath the surface, the structure of the Roman state did not change all that much as the Republic gave way to the Empire. The symbol of the Republic displayed on documents and monuments—SPQR, which stood for *Senatus Populusque Romanus*, "the Senate and People of Rome"—continued as the official mark of the Empire. More significant was the fact that the Senate and many other republican institutions remained in place throughout the years of the Empire. And though they lost much or all of their earlier authority, they, along with the Roman legal system, constituted the foundation on which the emperors based their own authority.

*A nineteenth-century engraving shows the second-century* A.D. *emperor Trajan being approached by citizens requesting audiences. The emperors maintained their power partly by appeasing the people.*

# A CIVILIZATION UPHELD BY LAW

In this beautifully worded excerpt from her classic book *The Roman Way*, the late historian Edith Hamilton summarizes the momentous achievement of Roman law.

"Over the lawless earth where petty tribes were forever fighting other petty tribes for the right to live, where there was nothing more enlightened than tribal customs untold ages old, marched the Roman, bringing with him as certainly as his sword and his lance his idea of an ordered life in which no man and no tribe was free, but all bound to obey an impersonal, absolute authority which imposed the necessity of self-controlled action. Along with the tremendous Roman roads and aqueducts went the ideal of which they were the symbol, civilization founded and upheld by law. The conception was magnificent, grandiose. It was Rome who spread wherever she went the great idea that a man must be assumed to be innocent until he was proved to be guilty; who pronounced it the height of injustice to carry any law out . . . without regard to the practical good or ill which resulted."

Thus, the emperor, though very powerful, could not seriously abuse his authority, for to do so meant going against centuries of cherished tradition and also a huge body of accepted laws. In theory, the people were willing to accept his authority as long as he lived up to his own responsibilities as the state's best possible citizen (*optimus princeps*, from which the term "best of princes" later developed). These responsibilities, scholar Harold Mattingly writes, were to be

pious in the service of the gods, just in his dealings with his subjects, strong and victorious in the face of the enemy, but merciful after victory; he must be temperate and kind, and . . . love peace and concord, those precious gifts without which states collapse into decay.[55]

Accordingly, most of the few emperors who did lapse into tyranny, notorious characters like Caligula (reigned 37–41), Nero, Domitian (81–96), and Commodus (180–192), provoked public outrage, had short reigns, and met violent ends.

On the whole, though, the quality of governmental leaders was usually not a major concern for the average Roman; in truth, throughout most of Roman history the common masses had little real say in government. The concept that concerned them most and that most affected their everyday lives was that of receiving fair treatment under the majestic protective umbrella of Roman law. Indeed, the great body of Roman law was the main structural link between the Republic and the Empire, preserving the best of the political and legal tradition of us) was that written laws should reflect naturally existing principles of justice that apply to all citizens within a state. Their first application of this and other rational legal concepts occurred in about 450 B.C., when they wrote down their first set of laws in the famous "Twelve Tables." These, like many other laws that followed, emphasized individual citizens' rights, especially rights pertaining to the ownership of property. For instance, one such law stated, "Should a tree on a neighbor's farm be bent crooked by the wind and lean over your farm, you may . . . take legal action for the removal of that tree."[56]

Later laws, which developed and altered as social conditions warranted, dealt with inheritance, women's rights, money matters, masters versus slaves, and many other issues, even including moral behavior. But all of them, right down to the Empire's last years, continued to use the original laws in the Twelve Tables as precedents. This was a prime example of Roman society's characteristic focus on the past rather than the future, on tradition and preservation rather than innovation.

*Caligula, depicted here, proved to be a demented and cruel ruler and was assassinated for it.*

Rome's past while continually growing and adapting to the needs and demands of changing times.

Above all, Roman law was based on common sense and practical ideas. What seemed very obvious to the Romans (and still does to

# CHAPTER FIVE

# FROM PLANTING CROPS TO CHARIOT RACING: ASPECTS OF DAILY LIFE

The nature and details of daily life for the average Roman varied, of course, depending on where the person lived. A farmer's life in the countryside was obviously quite different from that of a city dweller, who did not work the land and had more immediate access to markets, shops, temples, and games facilities. Similarly, merchants and sailors engaged in trade and long-range commerce inhabited another separate sphere with its own unique daily and yearly routines. (On the other hand, some aspects of daily life, such as the practice of religion, were common to almost everyone, no matter where they lived and worked.)

Daily life also varied according to the era in which people lived. In Rome's earliest centuries, for example, almost all men were farmers, and city life and commerce were not yet well developed. For the most part, the following pages describe selected aspects of life in late republican and early imperial times, when Roman civilization was at its height.

## Farmers and Crops

Because Rome had originally begun as a farming society and agriculture remained al-

ways the main basis of its economy, urban and rural Romans alike had a strong emotional attachment to country life. According to scholar Garry Wills,

> Romans always had a sharp nostalgia for the fields. Even their worst poets surpass themselves when a landscape is to be described. And all of them associated morality with simplicity, simplicity with the countryside. The city was foul, the country pure.[57]

Indeed, Virgil and other Augustan poets captured the perceived virtues of pastoral life in many of their works. However, their idyllic views of the fields were largely those of the members of the upper classes, who did not have to work in them. The harsher reality was that the vast majority of rural people were poor farmers, whose lives consisted mainly of long hours, weeks, and years of backbreaking toil for which material rewards were few and meager.

With the help of his wife, children, and sometimes a slave or hired hand if he could

*A Roman farmer herds the oxen that will pull his plow. Donkeys were sometimes used for the same purpose, but rarely horses, which were more expensive to buy and maintain.*

afford it, the average farmer grew grains, such as emmer wheat, to make flour for bread, one of the staple foods. Autumn was planting season. Using a crude plow (of wood, sometimes equipped with an iron blade) pulled by an ox, one person broke up the earth, while a second tossed the seeds by hand from a bag hung around his or her neck. Harvest time was April or May, when the workers cut the grain, then threshed it (separated the grain from the stalks by having horses trample it on a stone floor).

Usually, a farmer sold whatever his family did not eat to a *pistor*, a combination miller and baker who lived in a nearby town. The baker crushed the grain using a millstone, fashioned it into dough, and then baked it in a brick oven heated by charcoal. Archaeologists have excavated many bakeries (*pistrinae*) at Pompeii, which may have had more than thirty such facilities in all. In one, the bakery of Modestus, they found eighty-one loaves of bread still sitting in the oven where the bakers left them when they fled Vesuvius's wrath. Pompeii's bakers had their various specialties; one even made his own brand of dog biscuits from the grain he bought from neighboring farms.[58]

Grains were not the only output of such farms. They also grew vegetables and fruits, including carrots, radishes, cabbage, beans, beets, lentils, peas, onions, grapes, plums, pears, and apricots. These and other crops grew well in Italy and several of Rome's provinces, which benefited from the pleasant Mediterranean climate, consisting of short, mild winters followed by long, hot, and sunny springs and summers. The climate and soil were particularly favorable for growing olives, a crop second in importance only to wheat. Some olives were eaten. Most, however, were pressed to produce olive oil, which the Romans and other peoples used in cooking, as a body lotion, to make perfumes, and as fuel for oil lamps. Farmers also raised

livestock, including goats, chickens, geese, ducks, sheep, and pigs. They slaughtered some of these to eat themselves and sold the surplus.

In the first few centuries of the Republic, many such small farmers owned their own land, a typical holding consisting of two to five acres. But, over time, increasing numbers found it impossible to compete with huge farming estates (*latifundia*) covering hundreds or even thousands of acres. Owned by rich absentee landlords who lived in splendid houses in the cities, and utilizing the cheap labor of many slaves, these estates cornered the agricultural market by the early

*This photo shows the bakery of Modestus, one of several bakeries that prospered in Pompeii. At left is the opening of the brick oven and at right four round mills for grinding grain.*

years of the Empire. Some of the poor farmers who were driven out of business by the big estates migrated to Rome and other cities in search of work. Many others became poor tenant farmers who worked small portions of the *latifundia* in exchange for a share of the harvest.

## A Huge Volume of Trade Goods

While villages and small towns like Pompeii got most of their food from nearby farms, larger cities could not be fed on what was grown and raised locally. Large amounts of grain and other foodstuffs, as well as all manner of luxury goods, had to be imported, and that entailed shipping, trade, and commerce. The Romans quickly learned and exploited this concept as they expanded outward from Italy and won dominion over the Mediterranean world. By the early Empire, a wide variety of foreign trade goods, along with the agricultural and mineral wealth of Greece, Palestine, Egypt, Spain, Gaul, and many

*Thousands of Roman merchant vessels like this one carried goods to and from Italy.*

other lands, flowed steadily along the sea's liquid highway and into the Roman heartland of Italy. Indeed, that highway was the essential link that tied the Mediterranean world together.

The incredible breadth and diversity of this Roman trading network is well illustrated by a partial list of typical Italian imports: wheat from Egypt and northern Africa; spices, wild animals for the public games, oil for lamps, and ivory and citrus wood for making and decorating fine furniture also from Africa; copper pots and pans, pottery dishes, and fine wines from Spain and Gaul; gold, silver, tin, and horses also from Spain; glass artifacts and fine textiles from Syria; tin, lead, silver, cattle, and oysters from Britain; wool from the coasts of Asia Minor; linen and papyrus paper from Egypt; silk from faraway China; fuller's earth for cleaning clothes from the Greek islands; and magnificent statues and paintings from all parts of Greece. Amazed at how such a rich variety of goods from so many far-flung provinces and countries came together in Rome, Aelius Aristides remarked,

> If one would look at all these things, he must needs behold them either by visiting the entire civilized world or by coming to this city. . . . Here the merchant vessels come carrying these many products from all regions in every season . . . so that the city appears a kind of emporium [supermarket] of the world.[59]

The vast flow of goods into Italy was the largest but not the only aspect of Mediterranean commerce, for Italy exported products, too. According to noted scholar Lionel Casson, the Romans

# PIRATES MENACE ROMAN SHIPPING

Bands of pirates became a major threat to Roman trade and commerce during the early first century B.C. In this excerpt from his *Life of Pompey* (Rex Warner's translation in *Fall of the Roman Republic*), Plutarch tells how the famous general Gnaeus Pompey managed to rid the sea lanes of these marauders. In an incredible lightning operation launched in 67 B.C., his forces burned some thirteen hundred pirate vessels and captured four hundred more, all without the loss of a single Roman ship.

"The power of the pirates extended over the whole area of our Mediterranean sea. The result was that all navigation and all commerce were at a standstill; and it was this aspect of the situation which caused the Romans. . . to send out Pompey with a commission to drive the pirates off the seas. . . . Pompey was to be given not only the supreme naval command but what amounted in fact to an absolute authority and uncontrolled power over everyone. The law provided that his command should extend over the sea as far as the pillars of Hercules [Strait of Gibraltar] and over all the mainland to the distance of fifty miles from the sea. . . . Then he was . . . given power to . . . take from the treasury and from the taxation officials as much money as he wanted, to raise a fleet of 200 ships, and to arrange personally for the levying of troops and sailors in whatever numbers he thought fit. . . . He divided the Mediterranean and the adjacent coasts into thirteen separate areas, each of which he entrusted to a commander with a fixed number of ships. This disposal of his forces throughout the sea enabled him to surround entire fleets of pirate ships, which he hunted down and brought into harbor. . . . All this was done in the space of forty days."

sold abroad pottery and metalware and quantities of wine up to the end of the first century A.D. when [their] best customers, the provinces, began not only to produce for themselves but to export to their former supplier. In the second century [Rome] partially made up for this loss: marble had then become the popular material for public buildings and she shipped out large amounts from the famous quarries at Carrara [in northwestern Italy].[60]

## The Merchant Shippers

The cargo ships that carried this vast array of goods were wooden sailing vessels. The hulls were covered with pitch, an oily petroleum residue, to keep them watertight and painted with a mixture of soft wax and colored pigments. Judging from the remains of wrecks recently excavated from the sea bottom, most of these ships were about 60 to 100 feet long and 17 to 30 feet wide, and carried cargoes ranging from 50 to 250 tons.

A few cargo ships, notably those that ferried grain from Egypt to Rome for distribution to the urban masses or those that lugged heavy stone artifacts, were much larger. In A.D. 40, the emperor Caligula had a stone obelisk (the one that now stands outside of St. Peter's Cathedral in Rome) shipped to the capital from Egypt. The boat that hauled it was specially built to carry a burden of thirteen hundred tons.

The captains who piloted these ships had no instruments to guide them. For navigation, they relied on special nautical books that advised the best routes and sailing times and, particularly, on observations of the sun, moon, and stars. Also aiding them were many coastal lighthouses that employed polished metal plates to reflect light generated by bonfires.

Merchants and sailors were often away from home for weeks or months at a time. While docking at ports, they stayed in small inns (tabernae) with colorful names like "The Wheel," "The Elephant," and "The Rooster," which featured hard, uncomfortable beds but affordable prices. Merchants who traveled inland to and among the cities often stayed at guest houses called mansiones, which were located every fifteen miles or so along all main roads. Fortunately for these tradesmen, by the end of the first century A.D., Rome's extensive system of fine paved roads, covering Italy and the populated sections of the provinces, facilitated relatively easy transport of goods from one city to another.

## Education

Within the towns and cities that received the fruits of the Roman trade network, Romans of many walks of life enjoyed the benefits of a rich array of cultural and leisure activities. These included poetry recitations, the theater, various kinds of public games, and the public baths. For some, the list also included education, which unlocked the door to the special skills of reading and writing. Young boys and girls from families who could afford it went to a ludus, a private elementary school, which was supported by their parents rather than the state. (Children from most poor families were not able to attend school and usually remained illiterate; in fact, throughout Rome's history, a majority of Romans were either partially or completely illiterate.) At a typical school, which consisted of a single rented room, often in the rear of a shop, the teacher (magister) taught basic reading and writing skills to about twelve students at a time.

At about the age of eleven, girls generally left school. Some continued their education at home using private tutors, but most began preparing for marriage, which most often occurred when they were about fourteen or fifteen. Boys, on the other hand, went on to secondary school. There, they studied such subjects as geometry, geography, history, and music, and also learned to read and write Greek, since Greek civilization had such a profound influence on all aspects of Roman life. The primary function of secondary school, however, was to prepare young men for the study of rhetoric, the art of persuasive speech and public oratory. This skill was considered absolutely essential for the educated man, especially if he expected to go into law or politics, the two most prestigious professions.

Most of the reading materials used in schools, as well as most books, letters, treatises, and public documents used in society as a whole, were written on paper made from papyrus. This marsh plant native to Egypt was seen as vital. As the first-century-A.D. Roman naturalist Pliny the Elder put it, "Our civilization—or at any rate our written records—depends especially on the use of paper."[61] We know how the ancients made paper from papyrus partly because some surviving paintings show workers performing some of the steps. A few written descriptions have also survived, including a valuable one by Pliny himself, who says in part:

Paper is manufactured from papyrus by splitting it [the plant's stem] with a needle into strips that are very thin but as long as possible. . . . All paper is "woven" on a board dampened with water [to prevent the strips from drying out]. . . . The whole length of the papyrus is used and both its ends are trimmed; then strips are laid across and complete a criss-cross pattern, which is then squeezed in presses. The sheets are dried in the sun and then joined together.[62]

People wrote on the papyrus sheets with a reed pen dipped in ink made from carbon

*Among the many popular leisure activities in ancient Rome was attending the theater. Pictured here are part of the remains of the Roman theater at Orange, in Gaul (what is now France).*

*This is one of the rooms excavated in a bath-house in the buried city of Herculaneum.*

black (soot) and then rolled the sheets up around a wooden stick. Archaeologists have found numerous ancient Roman papyrus rolls in various states of preservation.

Archaeology has also revealed that the Romans wrote on other materials besides papyrus paper, including thin sheets of wood called "leaf tablets." A person either wrote directly on the wood using a reed or quill pen dipped in ink or covered the surface with wax and inscribed it with a metal pen. Recent excavations of a Roman fort at Vindolanda, in northern Britain, have brought to light more than fifteen hundred late-first-century-A.D. documents, many consisting of leaf tablets. In one, Claudia Severa, wife of the commander of a neighboring fort, addresses Sulpicia Lep-

idina, the wife of Vindolanda's commander:

Greetings. I send you a warm invitation to come to us on September 11th, for my birthday celebrations, to make my day more enjoyable by your presence. Give my greetings to your [husband]. My [husband] Aelius greets you and your sons. I will expect you sister. Farewell sister, my dearest soul, as I hope to prosper, and greetings.[63]

## Popular Leisure Pursuits

Some well-to-do Romans had private collections containing hundreds of papyrus rolls and other kinds of documents. But there were also collections of reading materials in public bathhouses (*thermae*), facilities that the Romans used for much more than just bathing. All across the Empire, people of nearly all walks of life paid regular visits to such baths, which could be found in every city and town. Public bathing was a major fixture of Roman life partly because most private residences were not equipped with formal bathing facilities; more important, the baths afforded opportunities for social fellowship and the exchange of news and gossip. Even the poor could afford to go often since the entrance fee was minimal (and children were admitted free). Most bathhouses either offered separate facilities for women or staggered their hours so that men and women attended at different times.[64]

The larger *thermae* were huge, beautifully decorated buildings featuring various hot and cold rooms and pools, saunas, and dressing rooms. They were also busy social centers where people conducted business, exercised, played games, and shopped. In addition to extensive bathing facilities, a large public bath housed massage parlors and hair salons; indoor and outdoor gyms, where people played handball and other ball games, lifted weights, and wrestled; snack bars and gift shops; gardens for strolling and leisure conversation; and reading rooms and libraries. Combining many features of modern malls and social clubs, the baths were places where people could enjoy themselves for a pleasant hour or an entire day.

Just as well attended as the baths were Rome's two most popular public entertainments—chariot racing and gladiatorial combats. The races usually took place in long oval-shaped facilities called circuses (*circenses*), the most spectacular example being the Circus Maximus in Rome, covering an area of some two thousand by seven hundred feet. Huge crowds of spectators (perhaps up to 250,000) attended. Just as today's football and basketball fans cheer on their home teams, Roman racing enthusiasts rooted for professional racing organizations represented

*The Roman baths at Bath, in England, shown here, are among the best preserved in the world. Most such bathhouses featured exercise and reading rooms as well as washing facilities.*

*A modern engraving accurately captures the great size and splendor of the Circus Maximus. This facility for horse and chariot racing held up to a quarter of a million spectators.*

by the colors white, red, green, and blue. And successful drivers—like Flavius Scorpus (first century A.D.), who chalked up 2,048 wins by the age of twenty-seven—became national heroes.

Today, large sections of the majestic Circus Maximus remain buried beneath extensive layers of dirt and debris accumulated over the many centuries following Rome's decline. The site occupied by the facility has been turned into an archaeological park, and excavation continues. The sheer enormity of the job, however, makes it an extremely expensive and slow process that will take at least several decades more to complete. Indeed, says scholar John H. Humphrey, "No single circus can be completely excavated during the working lifetime of one professional archaeologist if the excavation is going to be conducted according to the standards that are currently acceptable."[65]

Equally popular with the Romans were the gladiatorial combats (*munera*) and fights between men and beasts and beasts and beasts, which usually took place in amphitheaters like the Colosseum. To begin the battle, the gladiators raised their weapons to the highest-ranking official present and recited the phrase "We who are about to die salute you!" Then they fought, usually to the death. In other shows, "hunters" (*venatores*) and low-level gladiators known as "beast-men" (*bestiarii*) hunted and slaughtered animals, including tigers, bears, and elephants, to the delight of the spectators.

## Religious Worship

While the Romans came to see the baths, public games, and other leisure pursuits as highly desirable and fulfilling, they looked on another institution—religion—as essential. Religious worship was not only one of the traditional pillars of community life. It also provided guidance and comfort for the individual in his or her own everyday life. The relationship that developed between a person and the gods took the form of a sacred contract. It was thought that if a person observed the proper rituals—consisting mainly of sacrifice (of plants and animals) and prayer—the god being worshiped would react favorably; if the person failed in his or her religious duty, the god would become angry and perhaps exact punishment. The Latin expression coined to describe this relationship was "*do ut des*," meaning "I, the mortal, give to you, the god, so that you may give back to me."

At first, the Romans pictured the various spirits as natural forces rather than as formal deities. In time, however, some spirits began to take on human appearance and personalities. These became gods and goddesses, such as Vesta, goddess of the hearth; Janus, who watched over the doorway; and Mars, protector of farmers' fields. Over the centuries, as they came into contact with peoples more cultured than themselves, the highly impressionable and adaptive Romans incorporated foreign religious concepts and gods, particularly those of the Etruscans and Greeks, into

## THE HORSE RACES: CHILDISH AND TEDIOUS?

Public allegiance for Roman racing organizations, identified by the colors worn by their drivers, was often intense and sometimes even fanatical. Yet at least a few Romans were unimpressed. In a first-century-A.D. letter to a friend (quoted from Betty Radice's translation), Pliny the Younger tells why he detests the "childish passions" of the racing scene.

"If they [the fans] were attracted by the speed of the horses or the drivers' skill one could account for it, but in fact it is the racing-colors they really support and care about, and if the colors were to be exchanged in mid-course during a race, they would transfer their favor and enthusiasm and rapidly desert the famous drivers and horses whose names they shout as they recognize them from afar. Such is the popularity of a worthless shirt—I don't mean with the crowd, which is worth less than the shirt, but with certain serious individuals. When I think of how this futile, tedious, monotonous business can keep them sitting endlessly in their seats, I take pleasure in the fact that their pleasure is not mine."

# DID CHRISTIANS DIE IN THE ARENA?

Although firm documented evidence is lacking, it is likely that some early Christians were among those who were condemned to public execution in the Roman Colosseum. According to tradition, the first Christian who died in the great amphitheater was Saint Ignatius, bishop of Antioch, the first writer to refer to the church as "catholic," or universal. Supposedly, he welcomed martyrdom in the arena and exclaimed shortly before his death, "I am as the grain of the field, and must be ground by the teeth of the lions, that I may become fit for His [God's] table."

It should be noted, however, that the popular notion that the Romans were religiously intolerant and persecuted the Christians for having different beliefs is mistaken. By the mid–first century A.D., when Christianity was first spreading through the Empire, the highly tolerant Romans had welcomed and themselves practiced numerous alternative and often exotic religions from around the Mediterranean world. All of these flourished alongside Rome's state religion, which venerated traditional gods such as Jupiter, Juno, and Minerva.

What made the early Christians different was that most Romans viewed *them* as intolerant. In addition to condemning all other beliefs but their own, many Christians refused to acknowledge the emperor's authority, which disturbed the traditionally highly patriotic Romans. Moreover, the Christians kept to themselves, appearing to be antisocial, and over time acquired the terrible stigma of having *odium generis humani*, a "hatred for the human race." Worst of all, unfounded rumors spread that Christian rituals included cannibalism, incest, and other repugnant acts. Most Romans came to believe these fables and therefore felt little or no pity for any of the Christians who may have met their deaths on the arena's blood-soaked sands.

*The Christian martyr Ignatius, bishop of Antioch.*

their own faith. Thus, the Etruscan sky god Jupiter and the Greek head god Zeus merged into the Roman supreme god Jupiter. And the Roman field protector Mars became associated with and eventually assumed the same identity as Ares, the Greek god of war. Other important Roman gods that developed in Rome's early centuries were Juno, Jupiter's wife and protector of women and childbirth; Minerva, goddess of war and protector of craftsmen; Mercury, Jupiter's messenger, who protected travelers and tradesmen; and Apollo, the versatile deity of the sun, music, healing, and prophecy.

*A modern line drawing of Cybele, the widely popular "Great Mother" goddess.*

In addition to the cults of these and other major gods making up the sacred pantheon (group of gods) of the official state religion, the Romans came to embrace several eastern "mystery" cults (imported into Italy and the western provinces during the late Republic and early Empire). The oldest and most widely accepted of these was that of Cybele, the "Great Mother," from Asia Minor, a nature and fertility goddess. Other important mystery cults centered around Isis, an Egyptian deity whom the Romans associated with goodness and purification of sin; and Mithras, from Persia, whose followers preached treating all people with kindness and respect.

Another eastern faith that appeared in the early Empire—Christianity—had many elements in common with the others. Like Mithraism, for example, it featured the miraculous birth of a sacred baby, a sacramental meal of bread and water (or wine), baptism, and the promise of resurrection. Also, explains historian Charles Freeman,

> Much of the imagery of the New Testament—light and darkness, faith compared to flourishing crops—is similar to that found in mystery religions. . . . The development of the cult of Mary, the mother of Jesus, acquires a new richness when placed in parallel with the worship of other mother figures in these religions. . . . Many of the procedures of the mystery religions (initiation into the cult, for instance) were to act as important influences on Christian practice.[66]

Although Christianity was destined to one day become Rome's principal faith (in the late fourth century), it had to endure a long and difficult struggle to attain that status. In the Empire's early centuries, most Romans viewed the Christians as an antisocial, criminal element that posed a threat to society. This was, more or less, the rationale for the series of persecutions the Roman government carried out against the Christians in these centuries. For a long time, therefore, many Christians kept their beliefs a secret. Those that did not often ran a real risk of being excluded from the normal institutions and opportunities of everyday Roman life. And at times they risked worse—arrest and execution.

# CHAPTER SIX

# ANARCHY AND TEMPORARY RENEWAL: THE ROMAN REALM IN DECLINE

The series of events that historians refer to as the "decline and fall" of Roman civilization constitutes one of the most famous and important turning points in Western history. Unlike those great turning points that were fairly sudden, clear-cut, and easy to comprehend (for example, the French Revolution), the process of Rome's decline and fall was long and complex and is still not fully understood. This is partly because it occurred over the course of at least three centuries and had a number of contributing causes, the importance of each of which scholars still debate.

Moreover, Rome's decline was not a simple, steady downswing beginning at point A and ending conveniently at point B. For instance, the Roman realm suffered significant deterioration when it fell into near-anarchy in the third century, yet it temporarily bounced back in an amazing display of resiliency in the early fourth century thanks in large degree to the reforms and strong leadership of the emperors Diocletian and Constantine. Hence, it may be more accurate to

describe the various political, economic, and other crises and recoveries of the third and fourth centuries, in the words of noted scholar Averil Cameron, as temporary phases "in a developing and evolving imperial system."[67] Eventually that system *would* break

*A modern engraving shows a profile of the emperor Diocletian, founder of the Later Empire.*

76

down. But it is important to emphasize that the Romans of the third and fourth centuries did not realize they were in a fatal decline or that much of their supposedly eternal realm would soon cease to exist.

## The Anarchy

The first obvious signs that the Roman Empire faced serious problems occurred during the reigns of Marcus Aurelius, last of the "good emperors," and his immediate successors. This period of the late second and early third centuries marked the transition from the peaceful and prosperous *Pax Romana* era to what historians variously call "the century of crisis," "the anarchy," "the military monarchy," and "the age of the soldier-emperors." Whatever one chooses to call it, in the turbulent third century, Rome experienced a severe crisis that shattered its political and economic stability. In fact, at times it appeared that the Empire might collapse from its inability to deal with the prolonged onslaught of serious external threats and internal problems.

The external threats included violations of the realm's northern borders by Germanic tribes and full-scale war with the new and militarily formidable Sassanian Persian Empire, formerly the Parthian realm, on its eastern border. Among Rome's internal problems during the fateful third century was poor leadership. In contrast to the honest and able rulers of the second century, most of those that followed were ambitious, brutal, and/or incompetent. Another problem was a breakdown of military discipline, loyalty, and

*The members of a German tribe migrate into Roman Gaul. Such intrusions often led to war.*

efficiency, as Roman armies frequently ran amok, choosing and disposing of emperors at will. As the generals fought one another as well as foreign invaders, war and political instability disrupted trade, farming declined, and money steadily lost its value. As a result, law and order often broke down, poverty grew more widespread, and life in the Empire became increasingly miserable, dangerous, and uncertain.

Unable to deal with so many internal and external threats and problems simultaneously, Rome's military and administrative structure eventually buckled. The result was a period of near-anarchy, some fifty years of chaos and civil war that almost destroyed the Empire. On the political front, between 235 and 284, more than fifty rulers claimed the throne, only half of whom were legally recognized, and all but one died by assassination or other violent means. Meanwhile, in the wake of their ambitions, power struggles, and battles with foreign enemies, hundreds of Roman villages and towns were ransacked and in some cases totally destroyed.

# WHY AND HOW ARCHAEOLOGISTS USE AIR PHOTOGRAPHY

In this excerpt from *The Visible Past*, noted historian Michael Grant discusses a modern archaeological tool that has significantly aided the study of ancient Roman civilization—air photography.

"Air photography . . . heads the archaeological methods which have yielded historical results during recent years, providing new data at an ever-increasing pace. This type of photography is, simply, an extension of the principle that a camera held over the head, or raised on a scaffold, clarifies the relationship between one detail and another. . . . Air photography can perform many functions. . . . First, it permits sites to be comprehended at a single glance. . . . Moreover, air photographs provide evidence of topographical [ground surface] changes over the centuries. And they discover sites . . . that were hitherto completely unknown. . . . There are various particular ways in which [such] photographs explain features and objects which, at ground level, are invisible or incomprehensible. For one thing, such photography, when undertaken in low sunlight, produces informative shadow-marks. And then again, [buried] ancient buildings . . . often show up . . . because of the different soil which has become established on top of their skeletal remains, with the result that the crops or vegetables growing in that soil also display differences, perceptible from the air. Thus, cereals grow to a greater height, and ripen later, above pits cut in buried ditches, and conversely, grow shorter, as well as yellowing earlier, over hard ancient material such as road surfaces or the foundations of walls. . . . The patterns of settlement that thus emerge often throw light on social and economic changes which the [ancient] literary sources have not disclosed. . . . Although these techniques were substantially developed by [military pilot] O. G. S. Crawford in Britain in the 1920s, it was in the 1960s and 1970s that they reached their culmination."

The brutal sacking of the prominent city of Aquileia (in northeastern Italy) during this period illustrates the beginning of an ultimately fatal pattern of destruction and temporary renewal that characterized Rome's last centuries. A combination of written and archaeological evidence shows that the city was badly sacked by a Roman army in 238. After demolishing all the trees and farms in the surrounding countryside, the third-century historian Herodian wrote, "The army passed on to the walls . . . and strove to demolish [them] . . . so that they might break in and sack everything, razing [destroying] the city and leaving the land a deserted pasturage."[68] In the years immediately following, the inhabitants partially rebuilt the city, but subsequent raids by Germanic tribes inflicted more rounds of severe damage. Then, in the late third and fourth centuries Aquileia recovered again, only to be totally destroyed in 452 by the army of Asian conqueror Attila the Hun.[69] After that, Romans from surrounding towns carted away the stones from the ruined buildings for use in new construction.

Today, therefore, mostly only the foundations of these structures remain; however, archaeologists can deduce what most were used for by their shapes and by utensils, fragments of paintings and inscriptions, and other artifacts found in the rubble. Numerous other Roman villages and towns that were also eradicated and long covered by soil have been rediscovered in recent years thanks to the archaeological technique of air photography. The outlines of buried walls and structures often show up on photos taken from high above because vegetation atop such artifacts grows differently than it does in undisturbed soil.

## Emergence of the Later Empire

As cities like Aquileia were sacked, emperors swiftly rose and fell, and invaders threatened, disunity and chaos appeared to spell the end of the old Roman world. However, beginning in the year 268, a series of strong military leaders took control of the Roman state, and in one of the most remarkable reversals in history, the stubborn and resilient Romans were able to regain the initiative.

In the span of about sixteen years, these rulers, including Claudius II, Aurelian, Probus, and Carus, managed to push back the Germans and also to defeat illegal imperial claimants in various parts of the realm.

With the Empire's borders under control and minimal domestic order restored, in 284 a remarkably intelligent and capable man assumed the throne. He was Diocletian, who, like Augustus had three centuries before, took on the arduous task of completely reorganizing the Roman state after a period of serious disorders. The new Roman realm that emerged under his guidance, which modern historians often refer to as the Later Empire, was indeed more orderly than the deeply troubled one that had recently almost collapsed. Yet the new Rome would prove to be, overall, a less prosperous, less optimistic, more regimented, and grimmer place to live in than the Rome that had existed before the anarchy.

*The emperor Aurelian, shown in this portrait, had a short but notable reign.*

Among the first of Diocletian's sweeping reforms was the transformation of the imperial government and court into an "eastern"-style monarchy similar to those in Egypt and Persia, where the ruler was addressed as "Lord" and people bowed deeply when approaching him. Diocletian also drastically overhauled the Roman economy. To make sure that goods and services continued uninterrupted, he ordered that nearly all workers remain in their present professions for life. In addition, he attempted to regulate prices and wages, believing that such an effort would keep inflation down and the economy moving smoothly. Numerous fragments of his famous edict listing official maximum prices have been discovered in the ruins of the city of Aphrodisias (in southwestern Asia Minor).

Perhaps Diocletian's most important reform was the reorganization of the Empire itself. Realizing that administering so vast a realm was too difficult for one man, he divided it in half. He himself took charge of the eastern sector, ruling from the city of Nicomedia (in northern Asia Minor), and appointed as ruler of the western sector, a general named Maximian. In 293, Diocletian further divided imperial power. He and Maximian each retained the title of Augustus and appointed an assistant emperor with the title of Caesar, creating a four-man combination often referred to as the "Tetrarchy." Another administrative reform overhauled the provincial bureaucracy. "Military and civil commands were separated," Cameron explains,

> and each province henceforth had both a military commander [the *dux*, or duke] and a civil governor. The provinces themselves were reduced in size and greatly enlarged in number

[from about fifty to one hundred]. . . . The aim was to secure greater efficiency by shortening the chain of communications and command, and in so doing to reduce the power of individual governors.[70]

## Christianity's Triumph

Another hallmark of Diocletian's reign was that he was the last emperor to stage a large-scale persecution of the Christians. Despite the ravages of prior persecutions, the Christians had persevered, and their ranks had continued to grow; by the year 300 they made up somewhere between 2 and 10 percent of the Empire's population. Because they practiced inhumation rather than cremation (as most other Romans did), the Christians had come to bury their dead in underground cemeteries called catacombs. Initial excavations in the late 1550s and more extensive and professional archaeological examination in the late 1800s revealed the existence of extensive catacombs beneath Rome. Because these subterranean chambers were also used for religious services and decorated with art and inscriptions, they provide scholars with valuable information about early Christian prayers and rituals.

These prayers and rituals, long held mostly in secret, began to reach a much wider audience thanks to the efforts of the emperor Constantine I, later called "the Great" (reigned 307– 337). In 312, as he led his army toward Rome to unseat a false claimant to the throne, he supposedly had a dream in which he was instructed to have his soldiers paint a Christian emblem on their shields.[71] Constantine gave this order, and the next day, at Rome's Milvian Bridge, he annihilated his rival's forces.

*A fanciful modern drawing shows Constantine's supposed vision of a celestial cross.*

Crediting his victory to the Christian god, thereafter Constantine became a strong supporter of Christianity. In 313, he and Licinius, then the eastern emperor, jointly issued The Edict of Milan, which guaranteed absolute toleration of the Christians and provided for the restoration of all of the property they had lost in the persecutions. Later, in 322, Constantine erected the first version of St. Peter's Basilica (now the central structure of the Vatican in Rome, the residence of the Catholic pope). In 1939, while digging in the building's cellar, workmen discovered the floor of Constantine's original basilica. And beneath that, archaeologists uncovered a small shrine containing the bones of a man. According to Paul MacKendrick, the shrine

penetrated above the pavement of Old St. Peter's and formed its architectural focus. The conclusion is inevitable that Constantine in A.D. 322 planned his basilica to rise just here, at great trouble and expense, because he believed the lowest niche [of a wall in a cemetery that originally occupied the site] . . . to enshrine a relic of overarching importance, nothing less than the bones of St. Peter. There is thus no doubt whatever . . . that the [shrine] was reverenced in the fourth century as marking the burial place of the founder of the Roman church [although these may not actually have been the remains of St. Peter, who died in the first century].[72]

Thanks to Constantine's unwavering support, the Christians, though still constituting a minority of Rome's population, now had a firm foothold in its religious and political spheres. His three sons—Constantine II, Constantius II, and Constans—were all pious and committed Christians. They confirmed and extended the privileges their father had given Christian clergymen and made bishops immune from prosecution by secular courts, allowing them to be tried by their fellow bishops. By the 360s and 370s, the growth of the faith had greatly accelerated, and paganism (non-Christian beliefs) now found itself increasingly under attack by zealous Christian bishops. Under the persuasive influence of one of them, Ambrose of Milan, the emperor Theodosius I (ruled the east 379–391 and both east and west 392–395) abolished all pagan sacrifices and cults and officially closed all pagan temples. (Some temples were demolished, others were

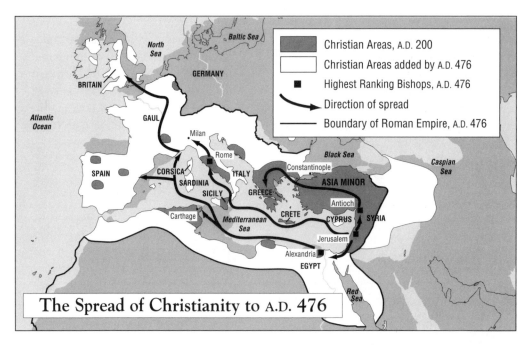

## The Spread of Christianity to A.D. 476

turned into museums, and still others were transformed into Christian churches.)

At this juncture, the number of pagans in the Empire remained large and their rituals continued in secret (ironically the opposite of the situation that had prevailed when the pagans were persecuting the Christians). But many of them must have realized that their days were numbered, for Christianity undeniably had triumphed. In astonishingly little time, the church, adeptly capitalizing on the boost Constantine had given it, had managed to achieve a controlling influence over the political and religious apparatus of the Roman state.

## Catastrophe at Adrianople

Another of Constantine's achievements that was to have major and lasting effects on the Roman Empire was his establishment of a new Roman capital in the Empire's eastern sector, which was more populous and pros-

perous than the western sector. The inauguration of Constantinople (the "City of Constantine") on May 11, 330, was important for two reasons. First, it was a Christian rather than pagan city from the outset, and this did much to legitimize and strengthen Christianity. Second, it marked the beginning of what would become a permanent division of the Roman world into western and eastern spheres, which over time would grow increasingly distant and distinct from each other.

Meanwhile, in the decades following Constantine's death, while the faith he championed was growing by leaps and bounds, the pressure by the barbarian tribes on the northern borders was increasing. Around 370, the Huns, a fierce nomadic people from central Asia, swept into eastern Europe, driving the Goths and other Germanic peoples into the Roman border provinces. "The Huns were indubitably [undeniably] frightening," writes historian Justine Randers-Pehrson, not only because of their Mongoloid features, their wild clothing, and their language that practically no one understood. Also frightening was their ability to dart around with lightning speed, which must have multiplied their actual numbers in the minds of their alarmed adversaries.[73]

The Huns' advance set in motion the greatest migrations of peoples in history, as the Goths, Vandals, Franks, Angles, Saxons, and many other tribes spread over Europe in search of new lands. As many as 200,000 members

of one branch of the Goths, the Visigoths (meaning "wise Goths"), poured across the Danube into Rome's northeastern provinces. The eastern emperor, Valens, allowed these refugees to settle, perhaps hoping to recruit their warriors for his army. However, his representatives unwisely insulted and tried to exploit the Visigoths, who responded by pillaging the province of Thrace (in extreme northern Greece).

Valens hastened with an army to put down this uprising. But instead of waiting for reinforcements from his nephew, the western emperor Gratian, he imprudently attacked the much larger enemy force on

## ROMAN BASILICAS TRANSFORMED INTO CHRISTIAN CHURCHES

One of the most visible changes in Roman life in the fourth and fifth centuries was the rapid proliferation of Christian churches, as summarized here by historian Charles Freeman (in his *World of the Romans*).

"Early Christian communities were forced to meet in private houses. . . . By the 3rd century, with numbers of converts growing, a whole house might be adopted as a church, with a large meeting room and separate rooms for baptism and clergy. . . . Once Constantine's Edict of Milan proclaimed toleration . . . for Christianity . . . this all changed. The emperor poured vast sums of money into his church building program and all over the Empire new churches appeared, resplendent with their fine decoration. . . . Many were built over the shrines of martyrs, places which had been venerated since the early days of the church. Others took over prime sites within the major cities. . . . Churches now became magnificent treasure houses, objects of awe and inspiration of worship. . . . [For their design] there was a pagan model to copy: the basilica, typically a long hall with a flat timber roof and aisles running along its length. For centuries the basilicas had been used as law courts . . . or [as] places to meet and gossip. Now they were to receive a new function."

*Vandal warriors like those depicted in this woodcut sacked Rome in* A.D. *455.*

his own near Adrianople, in eastern Thrace. On that dark day for Rome, August 9, 378, the overconfident Valens died, along with at least two-thirds of his army, perhaps as many as forty thousand men. When news of the catastrophe reached Italy, Ambrose called it "the massacre of all humanity, the end of the world."[74] The bishop had exaggerated, of course, for this one defeat, though crippling, was not enough to bring down the Empire. Yet his words bore an element of truth. Partly because afterward the Roman army was never again able to regain its former effectiveness, the disaster at Adrianople marked a crucial turning point for Rome, the beginning of a military-political downward spiral that would eventually seal its fate.

# CHAPTER SEVEN

# INTO THE REALM OF LEGEND: THE FALL OF THE WESTERN EMPIRE

In retrospect, the battle of Adrianople in A.D. 378 provides a convenient chronological point to mark the beginning of the Roman Empire's final, century-long slide into oblivion. First, many of the Roman troops lost in the battle were never replaced, and a majority of the military replacements and recruits in subsequent decades were less disciplined and not nearly as well trained as those in prior centuries. The steady deterioration of the Roman army in the late fourth century and throughout the fifth century was one of the principal causes of Rome's fall.

Unfortunately for Rome, the decline of its army coincided with a series of large-scale foreign invasions of Roman territory. There had been periodic incursions by northern European tribes in the past, but they became much more massive and more frequent in the century following Adrianople. These invasions constitute another major cause of Rome's demise. Not only was the Roman army increasingly less effective in stopping the intruders, but the government periodically and unwisely struck deals with them. This process, in which various tribes were given pieces of Roman territory, steadily re-

duced the size of the realm and the authority of the central government. The effects of these and other interrelated factors would inevitably prove fatal for the Empire.

## Military Problems and Decline

The policy of making land deals with the barbarians began in earnest shortly after Valens's defeat and untimely death at Adrianople. Valens's nephew Gratian, still emperor in the west, appointed the respected army general Theodosius to succeed his uncle as emperor in the east. In 382, Theodosius negotiated a deal with the Visigoths, who had defeated Valens, allowing them to settle in Thrace permanently. In return for providing troops for the Roman army, they were free from taxation and could serve under their own leaders, making them "federates" (*foederati*), equal allies living within the Empire. This set an ominous precedent for the future. As Charles Freeman puts it, "This was the first time that an area within the borders of the Empire had been passed out of effective Roman control."[75]

Over the next several decades, one barbarian tribe after another acquired federate status in the western provinces, a trend that steadily weakened the western Empire both politically and militarily. On the one hand, the Roman government lost much of its authority over an increasing amount of territory. On the other, large numbers of warriors from these tribes joined the Roman army, which in consequence suffered a continued reduction in discipline and effectiveness. Modern scholars sometimes call this process the "barbarization" of the Roman military. It had begun on a much smaller scale in prior centuries when the Roman government had allowed Germans from the northern frontier areas to settle in Roman lands. The emperors had pursued this peaceful policy partly because they realized that most barbarian groups wanted to *become* Romans, not to destroy them. These earlier tribesmen, scholar Stewart Perowne explains,

> had no desire whatsoever to set up their own fragmentary states. What

*Theodosius I, seen in this engraved profile, was the last sole ruler of western and eastern Rome.*

they wanted was to enter the Roman state, the sole repository of civilization and wealth. If necessary they would do it by force; but if they could do it peacefully, and get paid for it into the bargain, so much the better. Thus we find an increasing military intake from foreign [barbarian] nations and whole groups of foreigners settled within Roman frontiers at their own request.[76]

Once these settlers had established themselves, they were more than willing to fight Rome's enemies, including fellow Germans. Roman leaders, always in need of tough military recruits, took advantage of that fact.

However, as the recruitment of Germans into the military accelerated, this policy began to take its toll, particularly in a loss of discipline, traditionally one of the Roman army's greatest strengths. According to historian Arther Ferrill,

> The use of Germans on such a large scale that the army became German rather than the Germans becoming Roman soldiers, begins with Theodosius. . . . His Gothic allies . . . began immediately to demand great rewards for their service and to show an independence that in drill, discipline and organization meant catastrophe. They fought under their own native commanders, and the barbaric system of discipline was in no way as severe as the Roman. Eventually Roman soldiers saw no reason to do what barbarian troops in Roman service were rewarded heavily for not doing. . . . Too long and too close association with barbarian warriors, as allies in the Roman army, had ruined the qual-

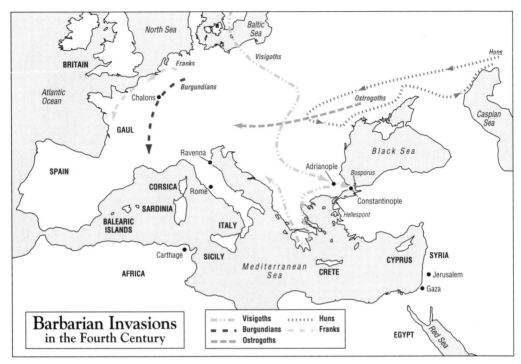

Barbarian Invasions
in the Fourth Century

Visigoths          Huns
Burgundians        Franks
Ostrogoths

ities that made Roman armies great.
. . . [By A.D. 440] the Roman army in
the West had become little more than
a barbarian army itself.[77]

A gradual breakdown in discipline was
not the only factor contributing to the ero-
sion of the Later Empire's military. The soldiers were paid very little and, because of the
government's frequent money problems,
their wages were often months or even years
in arrears. This damaged morale. Lack of
military funding, in combination with other
factors, also affected the quality of weapons
and armor. "By the end of the fourth century," writes Ferrill, "weapons and weapons
training had deteriorated drastically."[78]

In addition, the Roman army grew
steadily smaller, partly because of difficulties
in recruiting in the western provinces,
which were less populous than the eastern
ones, and also because some Christians re-

fused to fight. Perhaps the chief factor, however, was that many men found ways, either
legal or illegal, of avoiding service. Large
numbers of senators, clergymen, slaves, and
others were exempt from service. And because of low pay and the physical hardships
of service, some young men resorted to extreme measures, such as amputating their
own thumbs, to dodge the draft. When this
practice became widespread, the government at first ordered that such shirkers be
burned alive. Later, as the need for new soldiers became more desperate, the authorities
spared self-mutilated men from the stake
but forced them to serve in the army despite
their handicap.

## A Weaker, Poorer Government

Despite these many problems, the emperors
tended to welcome almost any recruits they
could find, partly because of heavy military

losses sustained in crushing a series of rebellions by imperial usurpers in the late fourth and early fifth centuries. The Empire also badly needed troops to deal with continued threats to the northern borders by various new barbarian groups. Because the soldiers had to be paid, all of these operations were tremendously expensive, and they drained the state treasury and other material resources, thereby weakening the government.

Meanwhile, some of the German tribes who had already come to terms with the government ended up posing serious internal threats to the integrity of the Roman state. One of the worst cases was instigated by the continuing division of the Roman sphere into two separate entities (begun by Diocletian when he set up a court at Nicomedia and escalated by Constantine's founding of the eastern capital of Constantinople). Theodosius, the last emperor to rule over both eastern and western Roman spheres, died in 395. His sons, Honorius, age eleven, and Arcadius, seventeen, assumed the western and eastern thrones, respectively; thereafter the governments and national policies of the two spheres became distinct enough to make Rome a *partes imperii*, an empire consisting of two independent parts. Naturally enough, each part was militarily weaker and financially less well off than the former whole, which did not bode well for Rome's future.

More immediately, this new political situation deeply worried the Visigoths. Apparently they thought that the deal they had struck with Theodosius shortly after the battle of Adrianople might be valid only under his rule. And now that he was dead and the empire permanently divided, they might be

*Alaric the Visigoth meets with the Roman general Stilicho in an effort to come to terms.*

vulnerable. So they banded together under a strong leader, Alaric, and began making demands. When the government refused to comply, they plundered Thrace. And a few years later, in about 402, they marched on Italy, where Honorius's army, commanded by the capable barbarian general Stilicho, momentarily halted their advance.

During that frightening advance, Honorius was rightly worried that Rome would be sacked. So he ordered the Aurelian wall, a defensive perimeter begun in the third century and added to over the years, to be heavily reinforced. In the mid–twentieth century, English archaeologist I. A. Richmond examined the surviving remnants of Honorius's additions, which included stronger bases for the original 381 towers built at intervals in the wall. Richmond discovered that Honorius's battlements were mainly defended by archers;

by contrast, in earlier times the Romans had mounted large artillery pieces (catapults and mechanical dart throwers) atop the wall. This reveals that by Honorius's day the increasingly impoverished government could no longer afford enough of the heavy-duty equipment it needed to defend the realm properly.

## The Sacking of Rome Shocks the World

Though Alaric and his Visigoths had failed to reach Rome, their bold attempt to do so turned out to have indirect effects that proved more disruptive and dangerous for the Empire than any attack on the capital would have been. First, to meet the Visigothic threat, Honorius had to recall several legions from Britain. Almost immediately, the tribal Picts of Scotland began raiding southward, while the Saxons and some other Germanic tribes crossed the North Sea and raided Roman British towns and farms. At the same time, en-couraged by Alaric's partial successes, another tribe invaded northern Italy. And in 406, fierce Vandal, Alani, and Suevi armies swept through Gaul, some of them continuing on into Rome's Spanish provinces. Stilicho managed to defeat the invaders in Italy. But because western Rome now lacked the resources to stop them, those who had entered Gaul and Spain stayed permanently. In addition, in 407, after the last legions were recalled from Britain, the island fell under the control of native and Germanic peoples.

With the western Empire seemingly in disarray, in 408 the stubborn and resourceful Alaric regrouped his forces and once more moved on Italy. This time, he was able to march straight to Rome almost unopposed. By this time Rome was no longer the imperial capital (which had moved to Ravenna, in northeastern Italy), but it was still the Empire's largest city and the chief symbol of more than a thousand years of Roman

*Alaric leads his Visigothic army into Rome in 410. The sacking of the city, repository of more than a thousand years of tradition and prestige, shocked the known world.*

## ROME'S SWAN SONG

This excerpt from the *Voyage Home to Gaul* (quoted in Duff and Duff's *Minor Latin Poets*) was composed circa 416 by the poet Rutilius Namatianus. Because it sings the praises of traditional Rome, suggesting that some Romans still held out hope for the Empire's survival and resurgence, the piece is often referred to as "Rome's swan song."

"Listen, O fairest queen of your world, Rome, welcomed amid the starry skies, listen, you mother of men and mother of gods, thanks to your temples we are not far from heaven. You do we chant [the praises of], and shall, while destiny allows, forever chant [them]. . . . Sooner shall guilty oblivion overwhelm the sun than the honor due to you quit my heart: for your benefits extend as far as the sun's rays, where the circling Ocean-flood bounds the world. . . . For nations far apart you have made a single fatherland; under your dominion captivity has meant profit even for those who knew not justice; and by offering to the vanquished a share in your own justice, you have made a city of what was formerly a world. . . . Spread forth the laws that are to last throughout the ages of Rome. Alone you need not dread the distaffs of the Fates. . . . The span [of Rome's reign] which remains is subject to no bounds, so long as earth shall stand firm and heaven uphold the stars!"

power and prestige. Surely, Alaric reasoned, threatening to sack it would force Honorius to meet his demands. These included making the chief Visigoth a Roman general, annually paying the tribe a large amount of gold, supplying the tribe with the food it needed to sustain itself, and settling Alaric's troops in some of Rome's key northern provinces.

When the Roman government rejected these audacious demands, Alaric besieged Rome and in 410 sacked it, an event that sent shock waves through the Mediterranean world. The noted Christian writer Jerome, who was then living in Palestine, spoke for many when he said, "My voice is stopped, and sobs cut off the words as I try to speak. Captive is the city which once took captive all the world. . . . The city of old . . . is fallen to ruin . . . and everywhere is the specter of death."[79] In reality, Rome had suffered relatively little ruin and death. Alaric's men had plundered much gold and other valuables but had stayed only three days and had done little physical damage.

Not surprisingly, many pagans blamed the great city's sacking on Christianity's denial of the traditional Roman gods. This charge motivated another renowned Christian scholar, Augustine of Hippo (later St. Augustine), to pen *The City of God*, in which he claimed that the pagans' own sins had brought about the disaster. Others looked to ancient prophecy for an explanation of the Empire's increasing troubles. According to one of the traditional founding legends, shortly before establishing Rome, Romulus had seen twelve eagles flying together; later generations of Romans passed along a superstition that each of these birds symbolized a century of the nation's existence. In the year 447, many noted, the twelve hundred years of the prophecy would be up. This, they said, might explain why the Roman world seemed to be falling apart.

## The Last Vestiges of Imperial Power

For those who accepted this ancient prophecy, the Empire's continuing downward spiral in the years following Alaric's plunder of Rome only confirmed their worst

*Augustine of Hippo (later St. Augustine), the most prominent and influential Christian writer of late Roman times, is shown with his mother in this modern painting.*

fears. In particular, the rise of an unusually fierce and powerful Hunnish king, Attila, in the 430s appeared to many Romans to signal the approaching apocalypse. By this time the Huns had built up an immense empire stretching from southern Russia westward across northern Europe to the Danube River. Living up to his nickname, the "Scourge of God," Attila ravaged various eastern and western Roman provinces for years, striking terror into the hearts and lives of millions. Luckily for the Empire, in 451 a combined army of Romans, Visigoths, and other German federates met and routed the Hunnish

*Attila, leader of the Huns, assures his troops that they will be victorious over the Romans.*

forces near Chalons (in what is now northern France). Two years later, Attila died unexpectedly and his empire swiftly disintegrated.

Like Alaric's sacking of Rome, Attila's rampages had clearly shown that the Roman heartland was increasingly vulnerable to attack. And sure enough, in 455, only four years after the great Hun's defeat, the city of Rome suffered the indignity of a second capture, this time by the Vandals. They had previously crossed from Spain into Africa, overrun Rome's fertile north African provinces, which produced much of the western Empire's grain, and gained federate status. (These actions had in no way threatened the livelihood and stability of the eastern Empire, which imported most of its grain from Egypt.) Now, with Italy seemingly at their mercy, the Vandals, led by their bold and capable king, Gaiseric, sailed north and ransacked Rome for fourteen days before departing.

The western Empire had by now shrunk to a pale ghost of the mighty state of the *Pax Romana* days. The last few western emperors, all of them weak and ineffectual rulers, reigned over a pitiful realm consisting only of the Italian peninsula and portions of a few nearby provinces. Even these lands were not safe or secure, partly because barbarian claims on Roman territory continued and also because what was left of the once powerful Roman army was fast disintegrating. The military situation in the northern province of Noricum, for which evidence survives, serves to illustrate a process that must have been taking place al-

# WHO WAS THE REAL LAST ROMAN EMPEROR?

It may be possible to argue on technical grounds that Julius Nepos, Romulus Augustulus's immediate predecessor, was actually the last official Roman emperor. As explained here by Michael Grant (from his book *The Visible Past*), the recent discovery of coins minted in the 470s seems to support Nepos's case. This is an example of how continuing archaeological research reveals new facts and thereby helps to reshape and refine our picture of the past.

"Nepos had married into the family of the eastern emperor Leo I, who helped him to secure the western throne. . . . His succession was confirmed by the Roman Senate and by some measure, at least, of popular support. . . . Nepos gave his principal military post, the Mastership of Soldiers at the Ravenna headquarters, to Orestes, formerly secretary to Attila the Hun. But when Nepos lost Gaul [to the Goths] . . . Orestes decided to replace him on the western throne by his own son Romulus "Augustulus." With this aim, Orestes led a force to attack Ravenna, whereupon Nepos . . . made his escape by sea and withdrew to his princedom of Dalmatia [on the western edge of the Adriatic Sea]. [Not long after Odoacer had deposed Romulus Augustulus in 476,] the eastern emperor, now Leo's son-in-law Zeno, received two ambassadors. One was from Odoacer, who urged formal recognition for himself in the West. . . . The other . . . came from Nepos in Dalmatia, who reminded Zeno of their marriage connection . . . and appealed for support to regain the western throne. . . . What happened next is revealed by the coinage. Although Odoacer . . . took no steps to invite Nepos back to Italy, he accorded him the recognition that the eastern emperor had requested. This can be seen by the gold pieces issued in Nepos's name by the mint of Mediolanum (Milan). . . . Odoacer also struck [gold] pieces in the name of Zeno . . . and in his own name. . . . As for Nepos . . . he was assassinated [in 480] by two members of his staff in his country house. . . . The last Roman emperor of any part of the West had now ceased to rule."

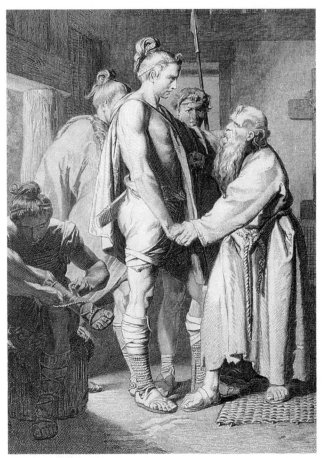

*The German-born Odoacer, depicted in this drawing, deposed the last Roman emperor.*

most everywhere in the west. "As late as the 470s," Freeman writes,

> there were still army units stationed in the main cities of the province. At one point their pay failed to arrive. One unit sent off a delegation to Italy to collect the money but no more was heard of it and the unit disbanded itself. Others followed and the defense of the frontier was, in effect, disbanded. Germans soon moved over the frontier to take control.[80]

Not long after the delegation from Noricum made its unsuccessful journey, Ravenna, refuge of the last feeble vestiges of imperial power in the west, came under German control. By this time, practically all of the Roman troops still active in Italy were German mercenary warriors, mostly Heruls, Rugians, and Scirians from eastern Europe, led by German officers. In the summer of 476, they demanded what Rome had granted to so many other barbarian groups in the recent past—federate status. Furthermore, they wanted one-third of the land in Italy in which to settle. The government refused, setting in motion the swift, final, and fatal chain of events. On September 4, their leading general, the German-born Flavius Odoacer, led a contingent of troops into Ravenna and without striking a blow deposed the young emperor Romulus Augustulus. No emperor took the boy's place, and the western imperial government, which had been barely functioning for decades, now simply ceased to exist.

When the news of these events spread through the rest of Italy, some noted with superstitious awe that the Roman state had lasted for a total of 1,229 years, a span almost exactly matching the twelve centuries of the ancient prophecy. Was this the work of divine intervention, either by the old pagan gods or the new Christian one? Or was it just a strange, perverse coincidence? No one could say for sure. What would become more certain in the ensuing years was that the Roman people and state would not succeed in rebounding, as they had so often done in the past. The city of Rome still stood, of course, and life for its residents went on as before for a while under German-born rulers. But the vast Mediterranean dominion that the Romans had once conquered with such boldness and vigor had slipped quietly into the realm of legend.

# THE
# LIVING TRUTH OF
# ETERNAL ROME

Although the old Roman government and its vast Mediterranean dominion passed away in A.D. 476, Roman culture was far from dead, both in the west and the east. Indeed, most historians stress Rome's continuity rather than its fall in the fifth century. Some emphasize that the eastern part of the realm survived as the Byzantine Empire for many subsequent centuries (until the Ottoman Turks sacked it in 1453). Others point out that traditional customs and a number of social institutions survived in the west for several generations after the last Roman emperor vacated his throne. According to this view, the change from antiquity to medieval Europe in the former western Empire was gradual rather than sudden. The late historian Ferdinand Lot summarized it this way:

> None of the great events, such as the invasions of the barbarians . . . the disappearance of the "Empire" in 476, the arrival of the Goths and their occupation of the country, affected deeply the social life or even the organization and administrative geography of the country. People imagine, or rather used to imagine,

some mysterious revolution in 476 which was not merely political but also social. . . . Things did not, however, happen in this way. . . . The [local] civil and financial administration functioned as before. . . . Rome was still the finest city of the West. The sight of it struck strangers and even the barbarians with admiration. It went on, moreover, with its life of idleness; there was no intermission of the circus and amphitheater games. It does not, in truth, appear that the Italian populace had to make any real changes in its habits.[81]

Stewart Perowne concurs, adding that the barbarian kings who ruled Italy in the late 400s and well into the 500s did their best to maintain a functioning government and to show respect for most Roman traditions and institutions. About the Gothic general who deposed the last emperor, Perowne writes,

> Odoacer deliberately maintained, even enhanced the established authorities of Rome. The Senate he regarded as his partner. . . . In 477 the record of con-

suls [that had been kept for more than nine centuries] had been interrupted: in 482 it was resumed. . . . Most significant of all, Odoacer showed every deference to the Pope.[82]

About Odoacer's successor, Theodoric, an anonymous Latin biographer wrote (circa 550) that he was

an illustrious man and full of goodwill towards all. . . . He gave games in the circus and the amphitheater, so that even by the Romans he was called a Trajan [one of the most constructive emperors of the *Pax Romana* era] . . .

whose times he took as his model. . . . He was generous with gifts and the distribution of grain, and although he found the treasury empty, by his efforts he recouped and enriched it.[83]

One should not infer from such enthusiastic accounts that Germanic rulers such as Theodoric maintained the old system in full flower for centuries. The fact is that the Germans did not absorb and perpetuate Rome's national spirit and ideals, which in any case had already significantly deteriorated in the course of the fifth century, well before the last emperor was deposed. Italy and other

*This European engraving effectively captures the drama, death, and devastation accompanying the sacking of Constantinople by the Ottoman Turks in 1453.*

*Theodoric the Great, who deposed Odoacer as king of Italy, proved to be an able ruler.*

former parts of the western Empire did undergo a major political, social, and economic transformation, but they did so slowly over the course of about three centuries. Thus, the year 476 should be seen as an evolutionary, rather than catastrophic, turning point.

The physical decay of the old Roman world was perhaps more apparent than the political and social changes were in these immediate postfall centuries. In the past, the Romans had routinely used stones from ruined buildings to build new ones; now the inhabitants of Italy and other parts of the former western realm began slowly but steadily dismantling intact structures as well. As Edward Gibbon lamented, the Romans eventually did more damage to their own works than any foreign invaders did. In Rome's final years, he wrote, its

monuments "were no longer revered as the immortal glory of their capital; they were only esteemed as an inexhaustible mine of materials, cheaper and more convenient than the distant quarry." In this way, to the constant regret of modern archaeologists and historians, the last generations of Romans "demolished, with sacrilegious hands, the labors of their ancestors."[84]

## Rome's Heritage to Later Ages

What people could *not* demolish was Rome's cultural heritage, which was deeply imbedded in the thinking and everyday habits of European life. As the old classical (Greco-Roman) world gradually underwent the transition to the medieval one, this heritage was quietly and steadily transmitted to future generations of Europeans, and over the course of many more centuries it reached the modern world. Thus, in one sense Rome did not fall. It merely passed from the world of flesh and blood into the domain of thoughts and ideas. And in this way the arrogant old Roman adage of *Roma aeterna*, "eternal Rome," has become a living truth. "Rome's triumphs and successes were canceled by her [ultimate political] failure," comments noted scholar Solomon Katz,

> but what she accomplished in diverse areas of endeavor was not lost. In the long perspective of history the survival of Roman civilization, the heritage which generation after generation has accepted, is perhaps more significant than the decline of Rome.[85]

That heritage that Rome passed on to later ages is profound both in its scope and its influence. The contribution that Roman law made to European law courts and justice systems, including such concepts as trial by jury, impartial justice, and unwritten "laws of nature," is enormous to say the least. No less influential was the means of expressing these laws—the Latin language. Adapted by different peoples in different areas, Latin gradually developed into French, Spanish, Portuguese, Italian, and Romanian, the so-called Romance languages.[86] And even after it had ceased to be widely spoken, Latin survived as the leading language of European scholars, as well as the official language of the Roman Catholic Church.

Christianity itself, of course, is among the most important of Roman cultural survivals. It was born in a Roman province, spread throughout the Empire, and eventually be-came the realm's official religion. Later, as antiquity gave way to the Middle Ages, it was the church that became the chief unifying force of European civilization, influencing and often controlling most aspects of daily life.

Through the efforts of its monk-scribes, the church also performed the vital service of copying ancient manuscripts, thereby preserving for future ages the ideas and writings of Greco-Roman civilization. Indeed, as the modern nations of Europe began to emerge in the fourteenth and fifteenth centuries, their

*In the library-study (scriptorium) of a monastery, a monk illuminates an old manuscript. Christian monks copied many Roman manuscripts, ensuring their survival into later times.*

*The members of this modern fire brigade, like other firefighters around the world, are the direct descendants of the* vigiles, *the firefighters who saved lives and property in ancient Rome.*

cultures were at first fascinated by and then relentlessly and subtly reshaped by the classical works they had found stored on the dusty shelves of churches, monasteries, and libraries. Some of the ideas contained in these works became the principal inspiration for the Renaissance, Europe's widespread cultural flowering in those centuries.

## All Roads Lead to and *from* Rome

Meanwhile, even though Roman political power itself was long since dead, Roman political ideals survived among the Germanic kingdoms that grew on the wreckage of the western Empire. Katz points out,

Long after the living memory of Rome's centralized rule was lost . . .

the idea continued to have an irresistible appeal. The coronation of [the German monarch] Charlemagne as Holy Roman Emperor in 800 and of Otto the Great [another German ruler] in 962 are concrete manifestations of the persistent conviction that the Roman Empire had never perished and that imperial might had not decayed but had been transferred to other monarchs.[87]

Many other Roman concepts and institutions (or Greek, Egyptian, or Persian ones that Rome had adopted) survived Rome's fall and are today woven, often imperceptibly, into the fabric of modern life. Only a partial list includes banks, hospitals, the postal system, fire brigades, bakeries, hairdressing shops, glass windows, central heating, apartment buildings, public sanitation (including drainage, sewers, and public toilets), the social welfare system, historical treatises and novels, the theater, the circus (which evolved from Roman games and theatricals), and public education.

In a very real sense, then, Rome is a "lost" civilization only in the sense that its government and empire long ago ceased to exist. Much of the culture it had built by piecing together the best ideas from many other ancient nations was *not* lost, but has endured in a myriad of ways to the present. As the late historian Max Cary so aptly observed,

> Rome was the principal channel through which the modern world has entered on the heritage of the ancient. If "all roads lead to Rome," they also lead out again *from* Rome. For those who have learned to think beyond yesterday, Rome is the focusing-point of the world's history.[88]

# NOTES

**Introduction: The Surviving Evidence of a Great People**

1. R. H. Barrow, *The Romans*. Baltimore: Penguin, 1949, p. 204.
2. Ammianus Marcellinus, *History*, published as *The Later Roman Empire, A.D. 354–378*, trans. and ed. Walter Hamilton. New York: Penguin, 1986, p. 49.
3. Cicero, *On Duties*, trans. Walter Miller. Cambridge, MA: Harvard University Press, 1961, p. 75.
4. Quoted in Jo-Ann Shelton, ed., *As the Romans Did: A Sourcebook in Roman Social History*. New York: Oxford University Press, 1988, p. 47.
5. Maurizio Forte and Alberto Siliotti, eds., *Virtual Archaeology: Re-creating Ancient Worlds*. New York: Harry N. Abrams, 1997, pp. 180, 182.
6. Livy, *The History of Rome from Its Foundation*, excerpted in *Livy: The Early History of Rome*, trans. Aubrey de Sélincourt. New York: Penguin, 1971, p. 34.
7. Quoted in Garry Wills, ed., *Roman Culture: Weapons and the Man*. New York: George Braziller, 1966, p. 245.

**Chapter 1: The Founding of Rome: Legends Versus Evidence**

8. Varro dated events "from Rome's founding" (*ab urbe condita*, abbreviated AUC). The system that employs the labels B.C. ("before Christ") and A.D. ("*anno Domini*," meaning "the year of the Lord") was introduced by Christian scholars much later (in the sixth century). These scholars calculated that Christ had been born in the year delineated by Varro as 754 AUC and labeled it A.D. 1 in their new chronology. In their system, therefore, Rome was founded 753 years before the year 1, or 753 B.C.
9. Claude Moatti, *The Search for Ancient Rome*. New York: Harry N. Abrams, 1993, p. 13.
10. Historians now identify this age with the late Greek Bronze Age (ca. 1400–1150 B.C.), a time when the Greek sphere was dominated by an early Greek-speaking people whom modern scholars refer to as the Mycenaeans. See Don Nardo, *Greece*. San Diego: Lucent Books, 2000, pp. 23–30.
11. Virgil, *The Aeneid*, trans. Patric Dickinson. New York: New American Library, 1961, pp. 141–42.
12. Virgil, *The Aeneid*, p. 14.
13. Plutarch, *Life of Romulus*, in *Lives of the Noble Grecians and Romans*, trans. John Dryden. New York: Random House, 1932, p. 31.
14. Livy, *The History of Rome*, in *Livy: The Early History of Rome*, pp. 40, 42–43.

15. T. J. Cornell, *The Beginnings of Rome: Italy and Rome from the Bronze Age to the Punic Wars (c. 1000–264 B.C.)*. London: Routledge, 1995, p. 60.

16. Cornell, *The Beginnings of Rome*, p. 32.

17. Chester G. Starr, *A History of the Ancient World*. New York: Oxford University Press, 1991, p. 457.

**Chapter 2: Rome's Early Centuries: Phenomenal Success at a Price**

18. Sallust, *The Conspiracy of Catiline*, in *Sallust: The Jugurthine War/The Conspiracy of Catiline*, trans. S. A. Handford. New York: Penguin, 1988, p. 220. Sallust attributed this speech to the famous politician-soldier Julius Caesar, although the wording is more likely the historian's own.

19. Quoted in Jane Gardner, *Roman Myths*. Austin: University of Texas Press and British Museum Press, 1993, p. 41.

20. Sallust, *The Conspiracy of Catiline*, pp. 180–81.

21. Livy, *The History of Rome*, in *Livy: The Early History of Rome*, p. 52.

22. Livy, *The History of Rome*, in *Livy: The Early History of Rome*, p. 61.

23. Livy, *The History of Rome*, in *Livy: The Early History of Rome*, p. 95.

24. Cicero, *Laws*, quoted in Naphtali Lewis and Meyer Reinhold, eds., *Roman Civilization, Sourcebook I: The Republic*. New York: Harper and Row, 1966, p. 380.

25. Cicero, *Pro Cluentio*, quoted in Michael Grant, *The World of Rome*. New York: New American Library, 1960, p. 100.

26. Paul MacKendrick, *The Mute Stones Speak: The Story of Archaeology in Italy*. New York: St. Martin's Press, 1960, pp. 95–98.

27. Michael Grant, *History of Rome*. New York: Scribner's, 1978, pp. 65–66.

28. The term *Punic* was derived from the Latin word *Punicus*, meaning Phoenician, the name of the Near Eastern maritime/trading people who originally founded Carthage about 850 B.C.

29. Appian, *The Civil Wars*, trans. John Carter. New York: Penguin, 1996, pp. 287–88.

**Chapter 3: The Blessings of Peace and Plenty: Rome Reaches Its Zenith**

30. The two major exceptions were the unbalanced Caligula (reigned A.D. 37–41), the first emperor to be assassinated, and the self-centered Nero (54–68), the first to be declared an enemy of the people. However, their reigns, though in many ways corrupt and/or ineffective, did no measurable harm to the Empire's overall prosperity.

31. Edward Gibbon, *The Decline and Fall of the Roman Empire*, ed. David Womersley. 3 vols. New York: Penguin, 1994, vol. 1, pp. 101–103.

32. Quoted in Donald R. Dudley, *The Romans, 850 B.C.–A.D. 337*. New York: Knopf, 1970, p. 139.

33. Dio Cassius, *Roman History: The Reign of Augustus*, trans. Ian Scott-Kilvert. New York: Penguin, 1987, p. 140.

34. Chester G. Starr, *The Ancient Romans*. New York: Oxford University Press, 1971, p. 104.

35. MacKendrick, *The Mute Stones Speak*, pp. 156, 160–62.

36. Michael Grant, *The Visible Past: Recent Archaeological Discoveries of Greek and Roman History*. New York: Scribner's, 1990, pp. 152–53.

37. Augustus Caesar, *Res gestae*, in William G. Sinnegin, ed., *Sources in Western Civilization: Rome*. New York: Free Press, 1965, p. 109.

38. Suetonius, *Lives of the Twelve Caesars*, published as *The Twelve Caesars*, trans. Robert Graves, rev. Michael Grant. New York: Penguin, 1979, p. 103.

39. Grant, *The World of Rome*, p. 234.

40. Barrow, *The Romans*, pp. 85–86.

41. Suetonius, *The Twelve Caesars*, p. 65.

42. Suetonius, *The Twelve Caesars*, p. 285.

43. Aelius Aristides, *Roman Panegyric*, quoted in Naphtali Lewis and Meyer Reinhold, eds., *Roman Civilization, Sourcebook II: The Empire*. New York: Harper and Row, 1966, p. 138.

**Chapter 4: Striving to Maintain Tradition: Roman Social Classes and Institutions**

44. Edith Hamilton, *The Roman Way to Western Civilization*. New York: W. W. Norton, 1932, pp. 111–12.

45. Michael Grant, *A Social History of Greece and Rome*. New York: Charles Scribner's Sons, 1992, pp. 49–50.

46. Grant, *A Social History of Greece and Rome*, p. 50.

47. Joseph J. Deiss, *Herculaneum: Italy's Buried Treasure*. Malibu, CA: J. Paul Getty Museum, 1989, p. 190.

48. Deiss, *Herculaneum*, p. 193.

49. Harold W. Johnston, *The Private Life of the Romans*. New York: Cooper Square, 1973, p. 31.

50. Cicero, *For Murena*, in *Cicero: On Government*, trans. Michael Grant. New York: Penguin, 1993, p. 123.

51. Leonardo B. Dal Maso, *Rome of the Caesars*, trans. Michael Hollingworth. Rome: Bonechi-Edizioni, n.d., p. 124.

52. It should be noted that the mere passage of these laws did not ensure systematic better treatment for all slaves. While the creation of such laws reflected the growth of humanitarian attitudes among Roman slave masters, it is questionable how many masters rigidly adhered to these rules; moreover, it is unlikely that more than a handful of those who broke them were actually prosecuted. For a detailed discussion of this and other aspects of Roman slavery, see Don Nardo, *Life of a Roman Slave*. San Diego: Lucent Books, 1998.

53. MacKendrick, *The Mute Stones Speak*, p. 260.

54. Darcie C. Johnston, *Pompeii: The Vanished City*. Alexandria, VA: Time-Life Books, 1992, p. 88.

55. Harold Mattingly, *The Man in the Roman Street*. New York: W. W. Norton, 1966, p. 104.

56. Quoted in Paul J. Alexander, ed., *The Ancient World: To 300 A.D.* New York: Macmillan, 1963, p. 204.

**Chapter 5: From Planting Crops to Chariot Racing: Aspects of Daily Life**

57. Wills, *Roman Culture*, p. 24.

58. Pompeii was also widely known for making and selling high-quality millstones fashioned from volcanic rock, which was obviously plentiful in the area.

59. Aelius Aristides, *Roman Panegyric*, quoted in Sinnegin, *Sources in Western Civilization: Rome*, p. 175.

60. Lionel Casson, *The Ancient Mariners*. New York: Macmillan, 1959, p. 226.

61. Pliny the Elder, *Natural History*, excerpted in *Pliny the Elder: Natural History: A Selection*, trans. John H. Healy. New York: Penguin, 1991, p. 175.

62. Pliny, *Natural History*, Healy translation, p. 177.

63. Quoted in Paul G. Bahn, ed., *The Cambridge Illustrated History of Archaeology*. New York: Cambridge University Press, 1996, p. 300.

64. This was at least the official arrangement; common practice was often quite different. Mixed bathing was introduced in the first century A.D. but banned again in the second century. Flagrant violations continued into later Roman times, as evidenced by the historian Ammianus's reference to mixed bathing in his *History* (see Hamilton translation, p. 359), penned in the fourth century.

65. John H. Humphrey, *Roman Circuses: Arenas for Chariot Racing*. Berkeley and Los Angeles: University of California Press, 1986, p. 4.

66. Charles Freeman, *Egypt, Greece, and Rome: Civilizations of the Ancient Mediterranean*. Oxford, England: Oxford University Press, 1996, p. 490.

## Chapter 6: Anarchy and Temporary Renewal: The Roman Realm in Decline

67. Averil Cameron, *The Later Roman Empire: A.D. 284–430*. Cambridge, MA: Harvard University Press, 1993, p. 12.

68. Herodian, *History*, quoted in Lewis and Reinhold, *Roman Civilization, Sourcebook II: The Empire*, p. 438.

69. The survivors fled to some nearby coastal lagoons, where they established a settlement that, in the centuries that followed, grew into the famous and culturally influential city of Venice.

70. Cameron, *The Later Roman Empire*, p. 39.

71. The emblem consisted of the first two letters of the Greek word for Christ, one letter superimposed over the other.

72. MacKendrick, *The Mute Stones Speak*, p. 345.

73. Justine Davis Randers-Pehrson, *Barbarians and Romans: The Birth Struggle of Europe, A.D. 400–700*. Norman: University of Oklahoma Press, 1983, p. 42.

74. Quoted in Michael Grant, *The Roman Emperors*. New York: Barnes and Noble, 1997, p. 264.

## Chapter 7: Into the Realm of Legend: The Fall of the Western Empire

75. Freeman, *Egypt, Greece, and Rome*, p. 507.

76. Stewart Perowne, *The End of the Roman World*. New York: Thomas Y. Crowell, 1966, p. 42.

77. Arther Ferrill, *The Fall of the Roman Empire: The Military Explanation*. New York: Thames and Hudson, 1986, pp. 84–85, 140.

78. Ferrill, *The Fall of the Roman Empire*, p. 50.

79. Jerome, *Letter 127*, in Leon Bernard and Theodore B. Hodges, eds., *Readings in European History*. New York: Macmillan, 1958, p. 44.

80. Freeman, *Egypt, Greece, and Rome*, p. 525.

**Epilogue: The Living Truth of Eternal Rome**

81. Ferdinand Lot, *The End of the Ancient World and the Beginnings of the Middle Ages*. New York: Harper and Row, 1961, pp. 237, 239.

82. Perowne, *The End of the Roman World*, p. 95.

83. *Anonymous Valesii*, quoted in Perowne, *The End of the Roman World*, p. 101.

84. Gibbon, *The Decline and Fall of the Roman Empire*, vol. 2, p. 374.

85. Solomon Katz, *The Decline of Rome and the Rise of Medieval Europe*. Ithaca, NY: Cornell University Press, 1955, p. 139.

86. Latin influenced other modern languages as well. For example, the Germanic tongues of the Angles and Saxons, two of the many barbarian tribes that overran the old Roman lands, eventually mixed with Latin and French to form the English language. More than half the words in English are of Latin origin.

87. Katz, *The Decline of Rome and the Rise of Medieval Europe*, p. 141.

88. Max Cary, "The Roman Empire: Retrospect and Prospect," in Mortimer Chambers, ed., *The Fall of the Roman Empire: Can It Be Explained?* New York: Holt, Rinehart, and Winston, 1963.

# CHRONOLOGY

## B.C.

### ca. 1000 (and probably well before)
Latin peoples establish small villages on some of the seven hills marking the site of the future city of Rome.

### 753
Traditional founding date for the city of Rome (as computed and accepted by Roman scholars some seven centuries later).

### 509
The leading Roman landowners throw out their last king and establish the Roman Republic.

### 201
Rome defeats Carthage, ending the Second Punic War, the most devastating conflict fought anywhere in the world up to that time. The victory gives the Romans control of the western Mediterranean sphere; in the century or so that follows, they will overcome the Greek states of the eastern Mediterranean, making that sea almost literally a Roman lake.

### 44
After declaring himself "dictator for life," politician and military general Julius Caesar is assassinated by a group of disgruntled senators, pushing the Roman world, already exhausted from a recent series of horrendous civil wars, toward more chaos and bloodshed.

### 31
In the Republic's last power struggle, Caesar's adopted son, Octavian, defeats his last rivals (Mark Antony and Cleopatra) at Actium, in western Greece, and gains firm control of the Mediterranean world.

### ca. 30 B.C.–A.D. 180
The approximate years of the so-called *Pax Romana* ("Roman peace"), a period in which the Mediterranean world under the first several Roman emperors enjoys relative peace and prosperity.

## 27

With the blessings of the Senate, Octavian takes the name of Augustus (the "exalted one"). Historians usually mark this date as the beginning of the Roman Empire.

# A.D.

## 98–117

Reign of the emperor Trajan, during which the Roman Empire reaches its greatest size and power.

## 180

Death of the emperor Marcus Aurelius, marking the end of the *Pax Romana* era and beginning of Rome's steady slide into economic and political crisis and eventually near-anarchy.

## 235–284

The Empire suffers under the strain of terrible political upheaval and civil strife, prompting later historians to call this period Rome's "century of crisis" or "the anarchy."

## 284

Diocletian becomes emperor and initiates sweeping political, economic, and social reforms, in effect reconstructing the Empire under a new blueprint. Historians generally refer to this new realm as the Later Empire.

## 307–337

Reign of the emperor Constantine I, who carries on the reforms begun by Diocletian; issues the so-called Edict of Milan, granting religious toleration to the formerly hated and persecuted Christians (in 313); and establishes the city of Constantinople (in 330), on the Bosporus Strait, making it the capital of the eastern section of the Empire.

## ca. 370

The Huns, a savage nomadic people from central Asia, sweep into eastern Europe, pushing the Goths and other "barbarian" peoples into the northern Roman provinces.

## 378

The eastern emperor Valens is disastrously defeated by the Visigoths at Adrianople.

## 395
The emperor Theodosius I dies, leaving his sons Arcadius and Honorius in control of a permanently divided Roman Empire.

## 410
The Visigoths, led by Alaric, sack Rome.

## 455
Rome is sacked again, this time by the Vandals, led by Gaiseric.

## 476
The German-born general Odoacer demands that the emperor, the young Romulus Augustulus, grant him and his men federate status; when the emperor refuses, Odoacer deposes him. Later historians came to see this removal of the last Roman emperor as the "fall" of Rome, although Roman life went on more or less as usual for some time under Odoacer and other barbarian rulers.

## 1453
The Ottoman Turks besiege, sack, and seize control of Constantinople, marking the end of the last surviving remnant of the Roman Empire.

# FOR FURTHER READING

Isaac Asimov, *The Roman Empire*. Boston: Houghton Mifflin, 1967. An excellent overview of the main events of the Empire; so precise and clearly written that even very basic readers will benefit.

Lionel Casson, *Daily Life in Ancient Rome*. New York: American Heritage, 1975. A well-written presentation by a highly respected scholar of how the Romans lived: their homes, streets, entertainments, eating habits, theaters, religion, slaves, marriage customs, tombstone epitaphs, and more.

Peter Connolly, *Greece and Rome at War*. London: Macdonald, 1981. A highly informative and useful volume by one of the finest historians of ancient military affairs. Connolly, whose stunning paintings adorn this and his other books, is also the foremost modern illustrator of the ancient world. Highly recommended for advanced or ambitious young readers.

Anthony Marks and Graham Tingay, *The Romans*. London: Usborne, 1990. An excellent summary of the main aspects of Roman history, life, and arts, supported by hundreds of beautiful and accurate drawings reconstructing Roman times. Aimed at basic readers but highly recommended for anyone interested in Roman civilization.

Don Nardo, *The Roman Republic* and *The Roman Empire*, both San Diego: Lucent Books, 1994; *Julius Caesar, The Age of Augustus*, and *The Punic Wars*, all San Diego: Lucent Books, 1996; *Greek and Roman Mythology* and *The Collapse of the Roman Republic*, both San Diego: Lucent Books, 1997. These comprehensive but easy-to-read overviews of various aspects of Roman civilization provide a broader context for understanding the leaders, trends, ideas, themes, and events of Roman history.

Jonathan Rutland, *See Inside a Roman Town*. New York: Barnes and Noble, 1986. A very attractively illustrated introduction to major concepts of Roman civilization for basic readers.

Judith Simpson, *Ancient Rome*. New York: Time-Life Books, 1997. One of the latest entries in Time-Life's library of picture books about the ancient world, this one is beautifully illustrated with attractive and appropriate photographs and paintings. The general but well-written text is aimed at intermediate readers.

Chester G. Starr, *The Ancient Romans*. New York: Oxford University Press, 1971. A clearly written survey of Roman history featuring several interesting sidebars on such subjects as the Etruscans, Roman law, and the Roman army. Also contains many primary-source quotes by Roman and Greek writers. For intermediate and advanced younger readers.

# Major Works
# Consulted

## Ancient Sources

Paul J. Alexander, ed., *The Ancient World: To 300 A.D.* New York: Macmillan, 1963. A fine selection of Greek and Roman writings, including excerpts from works by Livy, Polybius, Appian, Cicero, Suetonius, and others. Also contains the *Res gestae*, the short but important work written by Augustus (Octavian).

Ammianus Marcellinus, *History*, published as *The Later Roman Empire, A.D. 354–378.* Trans. and ed. Walter Hamilton. New York: Penguin, 1986. Ammianus is now considered the finest Latin historian produced in the Later Roman Empire. His honesty, balanced judgment, and elegant writing style rank him with the likes of Livy and Tacitus, to the latter of whom he is often compared. Unfortunately, only a few sections of Ammianus's history of Rome have survived, specifically those covering the years 353 to 378.

Appian, *Roman History.* Trans. Horace White. Cambridge, MA: Harvard University Press, 1964. Appian, a second-century-A.D. Romanized Greek scholar, wrote a history of Rome from about 135 to 35 B.C., which includes information on the doings of Marius, Caesar, and Cicero, as well as Octavian's (Augustus's) early career. Books 13–17 of the work are commonly referred to or published separately as the *Civil Wars*, covering in some detail the strife of the first century B.C. and fall of the Republic. A recent version is *Appian: The Civil Wars.* Trans. John Carter. New York: Penguin, 1996.

Leon Bernard and Theodore B. Hodges, eds., *Readings in European History.* New York: Macmillan, 1958. This collection of ancient, medieval, and modern writings includes excerpts from the works of Dio Cassius, Tacitus, Pliny the Younger, Eusebius, Ammianus, St. Jerome, Sidonius, and others dealing with the Roman Empire.

Cicero, *De Officiis (On Duties).* Trans. Walter Miller. Cambridge, MA: Harvard University Press, 1961; *Selected Political Speeches of Cicero.*

Trans. Michael Grant. Baltimore: Penguin, 1979; *Cicero: Murder Trials*. Trans. Michael Grant. New York: Penguin, 1990; and *Cicero: On Government*. Trans. Michael Grant. New York: Penguin, 1993. Cicero's works contain a wealth of information about first-century–B.C. Roman leaders (including himself) and the major political and social events of the era, as well as the attitudes and viewpoints of the Roman upper classes of his day.

Basil Davenport, ed. and trans., *The Portable Roman Reader: The Culture of the Roman State*. New York: Viking Press, 1951. A thoughtful collection of Roman writings from all periods, with especially large sections devoted to the poems of Catullus, Horace, and Martial.

Dio Cassius, *Roman History: The Reign of Augustus*. Trans. Ian Scott-Kilvert. New York: Penguin, 1987. An excellent translation of the parts of Dio's history dealing with the events of Augustus Caesar's (Octavian's) rise to power and reign as the first Roman emperor.

J. Wight Duff and Arnold M. Duff, trans., *Minor Latin Poets*. Cambridge, MA: Harvard University Press, 1968. Among the pieces presented here is the late Roman poet Rutilius Namatianus's *Voyage Home to Gaul*, part of which is a glowing tribute to Roman glory that has often been called "Rome's swan song."

Francis R. B. Godolphin, ed., *The Latin Poets*. New York: Random House, 1949. An excellent selection of short works by some of Rome's finest writers.

Naphtali Lewis and Meyer Reinhold, eds., *Roman Civilization, Sourcebook I: The Republic*, and *Roman Civilization, Sourcebook II: The Empire*. Both New York: Harper and Row, 1966. Huge, comprehensive collections of original Roman documents from the founding of the city to its fall, including inscriptions, papyri, and government edicts, as well as formal writings by authors ranging from Livy to Cicero to St. Augustine. Also contains much useful commentary.

Livy, *The History of Rome from Its Foundation*. Books 1–5 published as *Livy: The Early History of Rome*. Trans. Aubrey de Sélincourt. New York: Penguin, 1971. An excellent translation of these parts of Livy's massive and masterful history, written during Rome's golden literary age of the late first century B.C. Contains the most extensive available primary-source descriptions of Romulus and the Roman foundation.

Pliny the Elder, *Natural History*. Trans. H. Rackham. 10 vols. Cambridge, MA: Harvard University Press, 1967; and excerpted in *Pliny the Elder: Natural History: A Selection*. Trans. John H. Healy. New York: Penguin, 1991. Pliny's compendium of facts about the people, places, animals, and geological elements of his world is fascinating reading and also of great use to modern historians, even though many of the scientific conclusions he drew were incorrect.

Pliny the Younger, *Letters*. Trans. William Melmouth. 2 vols. Cambridge, MA: Harvard University Press, 1961; also translated by Betty Radice in *The Letters of the Younger Pliny*. New York: Penguin, 1969. The younger Pliny's letters provide an informative and interesting glimpse of Roman society in the first century A.D., especially the lives of the well-to-do.

Plutarch, *Lives of the Noble Grecians and Romans*. Trans. John Dryden. New York: Random House, 1932; also excerpted in *Fall of the Roman Republic: Six Lives by Plutarch*. Trans. Rex Warner. New York: Penguin, 1972; and *Makers of Rome: Nine Lives by Plutarch*. Trans. Ian Scott-Kilvert. New York: Penguin, 1965. We are indebted to Plutarch, a Greek who lived and wrote in the late first and early second centuries A.D., for his biographies of ancient Greek and Roman figures, including those of Romulus, Rome's founder, and various figures from the era of the collapsing Republic, among them Pompey, Caesar, Cicero, and Antony.

Polybius, *The Histories*, published as *Polybius: The Rise of the Roman Empire*. Trans. Ian Scott-Kilvert. New York: Penguin, 1979. This Greek historian's works are valuable for their often detailed coverage of the wars Rome fought against Carthage and the Greek kingdoms of the eastern Mediterranean during the third and second centuries B.C.

Sallust, *Works*. Trans. J. C. Rolfe. New York: Cambridge University Press, 1965; also, *Sallust: The Jugurthine War/The Conspiracy of Catiline*. Trans. S. A. Handford. New York: Penguin, 1988. Sallust's *The Conspiracy of* (or *War with*) *Catiline* is the most important source of information about the attempted military coup by the disgruntled nobleman Catiline, an episode that did much to shape the careers of Cicero and Caesar.

Jo-Ann Shelton, ed., *As the Romans Did: A Sourcebook in Roman Social History*. New York: Oxford University Press, 1988. Contains usable English translations of numerous ancient Roman writings, including poems, inscriptions, public documents, and excerpts from treatises and other longer works.

William G. Sinnegin, ed., *Sources in Western Civilization: Rome*. New York: Free Press, 1965. A fine collection of Roman writings, including excerpts from works by Livy, Polybius, Appian, Cicero, Suetonius, and others. Also contains Augustus's *Res gestae*.

Suetonius, *Lives of the Twelve Caesars*, published as *The Twelve Caesars*. Trans. Robert Graves, rev. Michael Grant. New York: Penguin, 1979. Suetonius's biographies of Caesar, Augustus, Nero, and other emperors contain much valuable information about these and other important Roman figures.

Virgil, *The Aeneid*. Trans. Patric Dickinson. New York: New American Library, 1961; also *Works*. Trans. H. Rushton Fairclough. 2 vols. Cambridge, MA: Harvard University Press, 1967. Fine translations of the writings of one of the greatest and most influential poets of all time.

Garry Wills, ed., *Roman Culture: Weapons and the Man*. New York: George Braziller, 1966. This excellent collection of Latin literature contains works by Virgil, Horace, Ovid, Plautus, Propertius, Martial, Catullus, Cicero, Juvenal, Lucan, Tacitus, and many other important Roman writers. Also, Wills's long introduction contains much insightful commentary.

## Modern Sources

J. P. V. D. Balsdon, *Life and Leisure in Ancient Rome*. New York: McGraw-Hill, 1969. A comprehensive, fascinating study of various aspects of Roman life by a noted scholar.

Peter Brown, *The World of Late Antiquity*, A.D. *150-750*. New York: Harcourt Brace, 1971. This important and influential book emphasizes the continuity of Roman life from the fifth to the sixth century, and the gradual, rather than catastrophic, transformation of the ancient world into medieval times.

Averil Cameron, *The Later Roman Empire:* A.D. *284–430*. Cambridge, MA: Harvard University Press, 1993. This well-written, somewhat scholarly volume contains excellent general up-to-date summaries of Diocletian's administrative and other reforms and of Constantine's reforms, including his acceptance of Christianity.

Jerome Carcopino, *Daily Life in Ancient Rome: The People and the City at the Height of the Empire*. New Haven, CT: Yale University Press, 1940. Long considered the classic general synopsis of Roman imperial customs, people, dress, food, games, religion, and much more.

Lionel Casson, *The Ancient Mariners*. New York: Macmillan, 1959. This very well researched and well-written study of trade, shipping, warfare, and other aspects of ancient ships, ports, and seamen is a modern classic and highly recommended for all.

T. J. Cornell, *The Beginnings of Rome: Italy and Rome from the Bronze Age to the Punic Wars (c. 1000–264 B.C.)*. London: Routledge, 1995. This well-written, authoritative study of Rome's early centuries offers compelling arguments for rejecting certain long-held notions about these years, especially the idea that the Etruscans took over and ruled Rome. Very highly recommended.

F. R. Cowell, *Cicero and the Roman Republic*. Baltimore: Penguin, 1967. A very detailed and insightful analysis of the late Republic, its leaders, and the problems that led to its collapse. Highly recommended.

———, *Life in Ancient Rome*. New York: G. P. Putnam's Sons, 1961. Cowell, a noted expert on ancient Rome, here offers a commendable, easy-to-read study of most aspects of Roman daily life.

Michael Crawford, *The Roman Republic*. Cambridge, MA: Harvard University Press, 1993. This is one of the best available overviews of the Republic, offering various insights into the nature of the political, cultural, and intellectual forces that shaped the decisions of Roman leaders.

Arther Ferrill, *The Fall of the Roman Empire: The Military Explanation*. New York: Thames and Hudson, 1986. In this excellent work, written in a straightforward style, Ferrill builds a strong case for the idea that Rome fell mainly because its army grew increasingly less disciplined and formidable in the Empire's last two centuries, while at the same time the overall defensive strategy of the emperors was ill-conceived.

John B. Firth, *Augustus Caesar and the Organization of the Empire of Rome*. Freeport, NY: Books for the Libraries Press, 1972. Beginning with Caesar's assassination in 44 B.C., this is a detailed, thoughtful telling of the final years of the Republic, including Octavian's rise to power during the civil wars and his ascendancy as Augustus, the first Roman emperor.

Jane F. Gardner, *Women in Roman Law and Society*. Indianapolis: Indiana University Press, 1986. An excellent study of women in Roman times. Highly recommended for those wishing to delve into some of the finer details of Roman life.

Michael Grant, *Caesar*. London: Weidenfeld and Nicolson, 1974. A fine telling of Caesar's exploits and importance by one of the most prolific classical historians.

———, *Constantine the Great: The Man and His Times*. New York: Scribner's, 1994. An excellent study of Constantine, his achievements (Christianity, Constantinople, etc.), and his impact on the Roman Empire and later ages.

———, *The Fall of the Roman Empire*. New York: Macmillan, 1990. Grant here begins with a general historical sketch of Rome's last centuries and then proceeds with his main thesis, that Rome fell because of many manifestations of disunity, among them generals turning on the state, the poor versus the rich, the bureaucrats versus the people, the pagans versus the Christians, and so forth.

———, *History of Rome*. New York: Scribner's, 1978. Comprehensive, insightful, and well written, this is one of the best available general overviews of Roman civilization from its founding to its fall.

———, *A Social History of Greece and Rome*. New York: Charles Scribner's Sons, 1992. Explores the ins and outs of ancient Roman social life and customs, including the role of women, rich versus poor, and the status of slaves and foreigners.

———*The Visible Past: Recent Archaeological Discoveries of Greek and Roman History*. New York: Scribner's, 1990. An information-packed synopsis of notable archaeological methods and discoveries relating to the classical world.

Harold W. Johnston, *The Private Life of the Romans*. New York: Cooper Square, 1973. An excellent, very detailed study of everyday Roman life, with an informative and useful abundance of Latin names, terms, and phrases, a feature often neglected in similar works.

A. H. M. Jones, *Constantine and the Conversion of Europe*. Toronto: University of Toronto Press, 1978. A superior general overview of Constantine's world and his influence, particularly in the area of religion, by one of the twentieth century's greatest Roman scholars.

————, *The Decline of the Ancient World*. London: Longman Group, 1966. [Note: This is a shortened version of Jones's massive and highly influential *The Later Roman Empire, 284–602*. 3 vols. Norman: University of Oklahoma Press, 1964, reprinted 1975.] An exhaustively detailed, endlessly informative work that touches on virtually every aspect of the history and culture of the Later Empire.

Paul MacKendrick, *The Mute Stones Speak: The Story of Archaeology in Italy*. New York: St. Martin's Press, 1960. Though now somewhat dated, this book remains an important and informative summary of Italian archaeological methods and finds in the nineteenth and early twentieth centuries.

Stewart Perowne, *The End of the Roman World*. New York: Thomas Y. Crowell, 1966. A commendable general overview of Roman history from Diocletian's reforms to Odoacer's removal of Romulus Augustulus from the Roman throne.

K. D. White, *Roman Farming*. London: Thames and Hudson, 1970. An informative discussion of Roman farmers and their methods, tools, crops, and lifestyles.

# ADDITIONAL WORKS CONSULTED

Lesley Adkins and Roy A. Adkins, *Handbook to Life in Ancient Rome*. New York: Facts On File, 1994.

E. Badian, *Roman Imperialism in the Late Republic*. Ithaca, NY: Cornell University Press, 1968.

Paul G. Bahn, ed., *The Cambridge Illustrated History of Archaeology*. New York: Cambridge University Press, 1996.

R. H. Barrow, *The Romans*. Baltimore: Penguin, 1949.

Arthur E. R. Boak, *A History of Rome to 565* A.D. New York: Macmillan, 1943.

S. F. Bonner, *Education in Ancient Rome from the Elder Cato to the Younger Pliny*. London: Methuen, 1977.

Ernle Bradford, *Julius Caesar: The Pursuit of Power*. New York: Morrow, 1984.

Keith R. Bradley, *Discovering the Roman Family: Studies in Roman Social History*. New York: Oxford University Press, 1991.

Matthew Bunson, *A Dictionary of the Roman Empire*. Oxford, England: Oxford University Press, 1991.

James H. Butler, *The Theater and Drama of Greece and Rome*. San Francisco: Chandler, 1972.

Lionel Casson, *Travel in the Ancient World*. Baltimore: Johns Hopkins University Press, 1994.

Owen Chadwick, *A History of Christianity*. New York: St. Martin's Press, 1995.

Mortimer Chambers, ed., *The Fall of the Roman Empire: Can It Be Explained?* New York: Holt, Rinehart, and Winston, 1963.

Gian B. Conte, *Latin Literature: A History*. Trans. Joseph B. Solodow, rev. Don P. Fowler and Glenn W. Most. Baltimore: Johns Hopkins University Press, 1999.

Tim Cornell and John Matthews, *Atlas of the Roman World*. New York: Facts On File, 1982.

Leonardo B. Dal Maso, *Rome of the Caesars*. Trans. Michael Hollingworth. Rome: Bonechi-Edizioni, n.d.

Joseph J. Deiss, *Herculaneum: Italy's Buried Treasure*. Malibu, CA: J. Paul Getty Museum, 1989.

Donald R. Dudley, *The Civilization of Rome*. New York: New American Library, 1960.

——, *The Romans, 850 B.C.–A.D. 337*. New York: Knopf, 1970.

J. Ferguson, *The Religions of the Roman Empire*. London: Thames and Hudson, 1970.

Maurizio Forte and Alberto Siliotti, eds., *Virtual Archaeology: Recreating Ancient Worlds*. New York: Harry N. Abrams, 1997.

Charles Freeman, *Egypt, Greece, and Rome: Civilizations of the Ancient Mediterranean*. Oxford, England: Oxford University Press, 1996.

——, *The World of the Romans*. New York: Oxford University Press, 1993.

Jane Gardner, *Roman Myths*. Austin: University of Texas Press and British Museum Press, 1993.

Edward Gibbon, *The Decline and Fall of the Roman Empire*. Ed. David Womersley. 3 vols. New York: Penguin, 1994.

Michael Grant, *The Ancient Mediterranean*. New York: Penguin, 1969.

——, *The Army of the Caesars*. New York: M. Evans and Company, 1974.

——, *Atlas of Classical History*. New York: Oxford University Press, 1994.

——, *The Myths of the Greeks and Romans*. New York: Penguin, 1962.

——, *The Roman Emperors*. New York: Barnes and Noble, 1997.

——, *The World of Rome*. New York: New American Library, 1960.

Sir John Hackett, ed., *Warfare in the Ancient World*. New York: Facts On File, 1989.

Edith Hamilton, *The Roman Way to Western Civilization*. New York: W. W. Norton, 1932.

John H. Humphrey, *Roman Circuses: Arenas for Chariot Racing*. Berkeley and Los Angeles: University of California Press, 1986.

Ian Jenkins, *Greek and Roman Life*. Cambridge, MA: Harvard University Press, 1986.

Darcie C. Johnston, *Pompeii: The Vanished City*. Alexandria, VA: Time-Life Books, 1992.

Solomon Katz, *The Decline of Rome and the Rise of Medieval Europe*. Ithaca, NY: Cornell University Press, 1955.

Lawrence Keppie, *The Making of the Roman Army*. New York: Barnes and Noble, 1994.

Ferdinand Lot, *The End of the Ancient World and the Beginnings of the Middle Ages*. New York: Harper and Row, 1961.

Harold Mattingly, *The Man in the Roman Street*. New York: W. W. Norton, 1966.

Alexander G. McKay, *Houses, Villas, and Palaces in the Roman World*. Baltimore: Johns Hopkins University Press, 1998.

Claude Moatti, *The Search for Ancient Rome*. New York: Harry N. Abrams, 1993.

Friedrich Munzer, *Roman Aristocratic Parties and Families*. Trans. Therese Ridley. Baltimore: Johns Hopkins University Press, 1999.

Don Nardo, *The Decline and Fall of Ancient Rome*. San Diego: Greenhaven Press, 2000.

———, *Games of Ancient Rome*. San Diego: Lucent Books, 2000.

———, *Greece*. San Diego: Lucent Books, 2000.

———, *Life of a Roman Slave*. San Diego: Lucent Books, 1998.

———, *Life of a Roman Soldier*. San Diego: Lucent Books, 2000.

Justine Davis Randers-Pehrson, *Barbarians and Romans: The Birth Struggle of Europe*, A.D. 400–700. Norman: University of Oklahoma Press, 1983.

Henry T. Rowell, *Rome in the Augustan Age*. Norman: University of Oklahoma Press, 1962.

Chris Scarre, *Chronicle of the Roman Emperors*. New York: Thames and Hudson, 1995.

———, *Historical Atlas of Ancient Rome*. New York: Penguin, 1995.

John E. Stambough, *The Ancient Roman City*. Baltimore: Johns Hopkins University Press, 1988.

Chester G. Starr, *Civilization and the Caesars: The Intellectual Revolution in the Roman Empire*. New York: W. W. Norton, 1965.

————, *A History of the Ancient World*. New York: Oxford University Press, 1991.

J. M. C. Toynbee, *Death and Burial in the Roman World*. Baltimore: Johns Hopkins University Press, 1996.

Mortimer Wheeler, *Roman Art and Architecture*. New York: Praeger, 1964.

L. P. Wilkinson, *The Roman Experience*. Lanham, MD: University Press of America, 1974.

# INDEX

# PICTURE CREDITS

# ABOUT THE AUTHOR

Historian Don Nardo has published many volumes about ancient Roman history and culture, including *The Decline and Fall of the Roman Empire*, *The Punic Wars*, *The Age of Augustus*, *Rulers of Ancient Rome*, *Life of a Roman Slave*, *Games of Ancient Rome*, and biographies of Julius Caesar and Cleopatra. Mr. Nardo also writes screenplays and teleplays and composes music. He lives in Massachusetts with his lovely wife, Christine, and dog, Bud.